AUGUSTE DE VILL[...] 1889) inherited delusic [...] from his father, who claimed, on highly dubious grounds, to be entitled to call himself Villiers de l'Isle-Adam and spent much of his life searching for the non-existent buried treasure of the Knights of Malta. He carried the imposture with him throughout his life, taking it with him into absurdity and abject poverty, but it doubtless helped to shore up his conviction that he was also a literary genus—which was, in fact, true, although the disorganization of his life limited the manifestations of the genius in question, the most important of which are the dramas *Le Nouveau Monde* (1880), *Axël* (published posthumously in 1890), the short story collection *Contes cruels* (1883), and the novel *L'Ève future* (1886). As is not unusual with literary geniuses, he received almost no reward while he was alive—hence the abject poverty—but he became world famous almost as soon as he was dead.

BRIAN STABLEFORD has been publishing fiction and non-fiction for fifty years. His fiction includes an eighteen-volume series of "tales of the biotech revolution" and a series of half a dozen metaphysical fantasies set in Paris in the 1840s, featuring Edgar Poe's Auguste Dupin. His most recent non-fiction projects are *New Atlantis: A Narrative History of British Scientific Romance* (Wildside Press, 2016) and *The Plurality of Imaginary Worlds: The Evolution of French* roman scientifique (Black Coat Press, 2016); in association with the latter he has translated approximately a hundred and fifty volumes of texts not previously available in English, similarly issued by Black Coat Press.

AUGUSTE DE VILLIERS DE L'ISLE–ADAM

I S I S

TRANSLATED AND WITH AN INTRODUCTION BY
BRIAN STABLEFORD

THIS IS A SNUGGLY BOOK

ISBN: 978-1-64525-004-3

Contents

Introduction

ISIS by Auguste de Villiers de l'Isle-Adam (1838-1889) was first published in 1862, in a small edition financed by the author, most of the copies of which were probably given away. It had been preceded by a volume of poetry, *Premières poésies* (1859) similarly self-published, and was followed by a drama, *Elën* (1865), which was not produced during the author's lifetime. The author continued writing, but remained virtually unknown outside of a small circle of literary acquaintances, where his reputation was that of an amusing eccentric, until the publication in 1883 of his short story collection *Contes cruels* (first translated into English as *Sardonic Tales*). He enjoyed a measure of celebrity thereafter that enabled him to publish the novel *L'Ève future* (1886; tr. as *Tomorrow's Eve*) and a few more collections of short stories, for which a glut of cheap newspapers provided a healthy initial marketplace, although he died destitute, in conditions of the most abject poverty, before rapidly becoming a legend and acquiring vast posthumous fame.

The dedication of *Isis* claims that the title in question is that of a projected series of philosophical novels, and the story that it contains, "Tullia Fabriana," is labeled "Prolégomènes" (Prolegomena, or Preliminaries).[1] Most bibliographical annotations therefore refer to the work as "unfinished," although that is not necessarily true. Insofar as "Tullia Fabriana" has a plot, that plot certainly leaves many loose ends dangling, and it refers continually to the heroine's mysterious plans for the future. One of several argumentative diversions in the text has a footnote saying that one item of discussion will be taken up again in the next volume. It is, however, possible to regard all of that as a literary device and to consider *Isis*, as published in 1862, as a finished work that merely feigns incompleteness as a part of its effect.

Further support for that thesis is easily provided by hypothetical examination of the question of how the suggested series might have been continued, and, in particular, how it might have been concluded. Tullia Fabriana is a kind of superwoman, not only awesomely equipped physically and mentally, and party to all the secrets of the Hermetic Tradition of occult lore, but has manifest supernatural protection from "Spirits" that have planned a destiny for her and solicit her obedience

1 In ancient Greek a prolegomenon was simply a prologue or introduction, but the plural term had been used by Immanuel Kant in *Prolegomena zu einer jeden künftigen Metaphysik* (1783; tr. as *Prolegomena to Any Future Metaphysics*) and was then bandied about freely by German philosophers, including Villiers's idol, G. W. F. Hegel, with reference to preliminary arguments laying groundwork for more intensive and focused analyses.

to their scheme.[1] It therefore seems unlikely that her projects would simply fizzle out and leave no historical trace, even though they are intended to change the world, apparently for the better. The story is, however, set in 1788. Any reader tempted to take the implication from that date that Tullia might have been secretly responsible for historical events taking place in between 1789 and 1862 would be confounded by the difficulty of arguing that such events have qualified as ameliorations even within the frontiers of Italy, the base of her operations, let alone the world as a whole.

The "future" to which Tullia Fabriana's story looks forward, and to which it is said to be preliminary, is, therefore, that of an alternative history, which did not actually happen, and it is therefore not inappropriate, esthetically, that it should be mapped out in a series of imaginary texts that were never actually written. It should not be forgotten, either, that the story was written under the Second Empire, when any further text going into detail regarding the reformist political plans nurtured by Tullia Fabriana and her guiding Spirits would undoubtedly have been suppressed by Napoléon III's censors.

---

1 Most readers would inevitably have construed the narrative's *Esprits* [Spirits] in the conventional sense of spiritual beings akin to angels, but, further to the last note, it is worth remembering that Hegel made elaborate use of the German word *geist* [spirit], often in such compound terms as *weltgeist* [World-Spirit] and *zeitgeist* [Spirit of the Age], in a rather different sense, and Villiers might well have had quasi-Hegelian ideas in mind when constructing the metaphysical backcloth of his narrative. The *Esprits* guiding and manipulating Tullia might, therefore, be the *weltgeist* and the *zeitgeist*.

The laces of the straitjacket in which French authors had been working throughout the 1850s had been loosened somewhat by 1862, but not sufficiently to allow any but the vaguest and most tentative political commentary into print without grave personal risk. Had that not been the case, the text of *Isis* could have, and perhaps would have, been more outspoken in that regard.

The conclusion toward which the narrative actually tends, therefore, is not the impossible future toward which it pretends to be heading. The numinous dream of world manipulation sketched out in the heroine's mind is exactly what it appears to be: a vague and unfulfillable dream. The true ending—the only possible ending—is the climax that the text actually attains, contained in an elliptically succinct fashion in its final line. All the rest is, indeed, prolegomena, in the particular sense of foreplay: a calculatedly bizarre collage of images and aperçus cemented together by a tokenistic story-line, purely for the purpose of the procrastination and intensification of literary pleasure. That, at least, is the way that the sensitive reader ought to regard the text, if only because it transforms the work from something incomplete, and hence only of partial and unsatisfactory interest, into a *tour de force* of extravagant implication and esthetic dexterity: a work of peculiar genius. What does it matter whether or not the interpretation is strictly true, given that the story itself is, in essence, a bizarre sexual fantasy?

Isis is not usually cited among the great classics of Decadent literature, but that is because its reputation as an unfinished work has put people off reading it and paying critical attention to it. It is certainly fragmentary and inconsequential, but that is a matter of deliberate artifice rather than flawed construction. It is the work of a young writer bursting with exuberance, more concerned with momentary effect and extravagant inclusion than continuity and order. Seen in context, as an intimate development of the pioneering labor done by Charles Baudelaire and Théophile Gautier in planting the seeds from which the *fin-de-siècle* Decadent Movement would eventually sprout and blossom, it deserves to be reckoned one of the foundation-stones of Decadent prose fiction, redolent with echoes of Byron and Poe, reconfigured in the Baudelairean manner, and flamboyant with Gautieresque elements, explicitly embroidering the themes of both of Gautier's proto-Decadent masterpieces, *Mademoiselle de Maupin* (1835)[1] and "Une nuit de Cléopâtre" (1838; tr. as "One of Cleopatra's Nights").

Being something of a patchwork, *Isis* seems to the modern eye only to feature and develop what Gautier had not yet defined in 1862 as "the Decadent style" in parts, mostly in the sections that deal with the architecture and décor of Tullia Fabriana's palace—especially the astonishing room in which the final scene takes place—and the analyses of her idiosyncratic species of ennui, also concentrated in the final chapters. Those

1 *Mademoiselle de Maupin* was written when Gautier was approaching his twenty-fourth birthday, the same age as Villiers when *Isis* was written. By the time that Villiers met him, Gautier was much older; so was Baudelaire, ten years younger than Gautier but seventeen years older than Villiers; both would inevitably have seemed to the latter to belong to a different generation, but nevertheless very much in tune with, and perhaps ahead of, the *zeitgeist*.

passages are, in fact, somewhat in contrast with the style and content of the early chapters of the narrative and that of the long diversion interrogating the theory of progress, but that heterogeneity, whether or not it is a result of the author's intellectual and esthetic evolution while he was compiling the text—perhaps not in the linear form taken by the printed version—it is, once again, something that can be seen as a matter of literary strategy rather than a flaw.

In any case, unlike the proverbial curate's egg, books really can be better in some parts than others, and none of *Isis* is bad, although some of its many eccentricities will doubtless not be as much to the taste of any individual reader as others; it is certainly spectacular in parts, although not all readers will appreciate its readiness to go way over the top whenever the opportunity arises. It is certainly a work given to excess, in its vaulting ambitions, its quirky mannerisms, its philosophical posturing and its lush descriptions, but that excess is the essence of the endeavor, the wand of its enchantment.

Rumor has it that in person, like Baudelaire, Oscar Wilde and Francis Crick, Villiers was never encountered in a modest mood; he was flamboyant, unpredictable, permanently deluded—notably with respect to the illusion of aristocracy inherited from his crazy father and preserved in his signature—and always eager to make an impression. His written work has exactly the same personality; *Isis* provided him with the first opportunity to express himself at length, sprawling in the chaise-longue of the novel rather than perched on the footstool of the short story or the tiptoes of verse, and he took gluttonous advantage of it. It was perhaps as well, as the only other opportunity he found came to him much later in life, when he is said to have written much of the oft-interrupted *L'Ève future*—two incomplete serial versions of which appeared before the definitive version was published as a book—lying face down on the bare floor of his largely-unfurnished room in order to make the best use of the light of a single candle, continually on the brink of starvation. Exuberance was then far more difficult to contrive, and bitterness impossible to avoid.

Even in 1862, Villiers had not been living in the hypothetical Revolutionary future glimpsed in Tullia Fabriana's spirit-assisted dreams, but in 1883 he was all too well aware of having fallen, metaphorically, into one of the dark pits reserved for ill-intentioned intruders into her private fantasy-world. In spite of that, however, he had not given up on his dreams or his literary aspirations. When he died he was still working on the drama that he had long intended to be his masterpiece, *Axël*, begun in 1869 and published posthumously in 1890, which carried forward some of the philosophical themes and reproduced much of the architectural and Romantic imagery of *Isis*; that work too is peculiarly ambiguous in regard to its completeness, finished in fact but not in its creator's imagination. *Isis* thus embodies and foreshadows a lifelong paradoxicality on the part of the author and his work, and represents a crucial piece of the jigsaw-puzzle of one of the most original, eccentric and unsteadily brilliant writers ever to set pen to paper.

Everyone nowadays tends to approach Villiers' work backwards, beginning with his later productions, and leaving *Isis* until last, if they bother to reach it at all. That is not entirely unfortunate—there is no right way to approach such a paradoxical figure except the wrong way—but it does not favor a full understanding or an accurate assessment of his work. Whether it is encountered first or last, *Isis* is certainly vital to any such understanding and evaluation, and this long-belated translation will hopefully assist English readers in that admittedly-esoteric quest.

✳

This translation was made from the copy of the posthumous edition published by the Libraire Internationale reproduced on the Bibliothèque Nationale's *gallica* website. That edition bears the date 1890, but the BN catalogue records its date of publication as 1900, which might or might not be a mistake.

—Brian Stableford

ISIS

"Eritis sicut Dii . . ."[1]
The Sepher.

---

1 "You will be as gods . . ." The quotation is originally from *Genesis* 3:5, although it is bound to be referenced in the Cabalistic document known as *Sepher Yetzirah* [The Book of Creation].

To Monsieur
Hyacinthe du Pontavice de Heussey,[1]

Permit me, Monsieur and very dear friend, to offer you this study in memory of the sentiments of sympathy and admiration that you have inspired in me.

"Isis" is the title of an ensemble of works that will appear, if I may hope, at brief intervals; it is the collective formula of a series of philosophical novels; it is the X of a problem and an ideal; it is the great unknown. The work will define itself once it is complete.

Believe, in the meantime, that I am glad to inscribe your name on its first page.

A. de Villiers de l'Isle-Adam.

Paris, 2 July 1862.

---

1 The Romantic poet Hyacinthe du Pontavice de Heussey (1814-1876), a friend of Baudelaire, was Villiers's mentor.

PROLEGOMENA

I

TULLA FABRIANA

Everything seems to announce that the present century is bound to see the most ardent and most decisive struggles that have ever been delivered regarding the greatest interests with which humans have the right to preoccupy themselves down here.

Dom Guéranger.[1]

---

1 The Benedictine monk Prosper Guéranger (1805-1875) was the Abbot of Solesmes Abbey, where Villiers once went on retreat. He played a leading role in the restoration of French monasticism after its obliteration by the 1789 Revolution. His day-by-day account of *L'Année liturgique* [The Liturgical Year] filled fifteen volumes.

Chapter I

Italy

THERE had been a soirée at the Pitti Palace.

The Duchess of Esperia, a beautiful woman of the most gracious distinction, had introduced the Count of Strally-d'Anthas to all Florence.

He appeared to be twenty years old at the most. He was traveling and came from Germany. His mother was from one of the most illustrious families in Italy; everyone knew that. He was therefore allied to the highest nobility in the land; the duchess was a distant cousin; there had been no difficulty in his being introduced by her.

Prince Forsiani, appointed the day before as the Tuscan ambassador to Sicily, had seemed to take an interest in him. He was an old courtier, fine and cold but solidly esteemed by everyone. In the measure of the indifference of society, he was sufficiently well-liked

After the customary respectful formulae, the young man had sat down at a chessboard opposite Lord Seymour, and a circle of amateurs and bored observers had surrounded the game. In the other drawing rooms there was dancing. Whispers were exchanged regarding the conduct of the young German, who was playing instead of dancing as befit his age.

Various currents of ideas were soon stirring vaguely around Prince Forsiani, the Duchess and Strally, whose fine physiognomy drew comment. What caused a sensation was the introduction of the young man to the papal legate—who deigned to arrive at eleven o'clock—by the Duke of Esperia himself.

His Eminence had been very gracious during that ceremony; it was divinable that there had been a recommendation. But why the Duke of Esperia's urgency? Was it not excessive?

An old lady insinuated to her intimate friends, between a smile and a mirror that the ambassador had known the Countess of Strally divinely in the time when she lived in Florence before her marriage to the Margrave d'Anthas. That was said in Italian. A second lady, similarly over forty, judged it apt to observe that the prince was not married. Those words comprised a sum of hesitations so profound that no one pursued them.

As for the young man, he simply continued playing.

Nothing significant was advanced, as might be expected, after those few words.

During the soirée there were another two fragments of conversation sufficiently worthy of note for what they implied. The nuncio and the Duchess of Esperia chatted in isolation, in polite voices, for a minute.

"And your Eminence has been there?"

"Oh, I'm sure that *She* isn't at the palace," the nuncio replied. "Nevertheless, as it would be very useful to obtain an auxiliary of that value, perhaps I shall leave a note on Saturday, in the case of a further absence."

"That's rather excessive, Monsignor."

An Italian smile glided weakly over His Eminence's lips as he drew away with a slight bow.

Prince Forsiani returned. To an indifferent glance from the Duchess of Esperia, he responded, affably but in a hasty and very low voice: "I'm departing for Naples tomorrow night. I'll take Wilhelm to the Casines at about nine o'clock in the evening. The meeting is fixed for ten."

"Fixed! You've seen her, then, the invisible beauty?"

"In the ducal drawing room ten minutes ago. She was alone with His Royal Highness and the Persian envoy. A few seconds later, she accepted my hand as far as her carriage. A few words sufficed."

Several cavaliers of brilliant and satisfied beauties intervened. The mysterious subject was left there. There were ceremonious felicitations, and toward half past two in the morning, everyone separated. The sound of carriages diminished, and the night became silent over Florence.

Chapter II

The Expected Man

THE next day, at nine o'clock in the evening, Prince Forsiani was walking in an avenue of the Casines.

Today, the Casines are the Champs-Élysées of Florence. One encounters statues hidden there in vast walls of verdure, rare animals, tall sculpted trees and foreigners from all lands. The castles of the Grand Dukes of Tuscany only date from 1787. In 1788, the epoch in which we are, there was rubble, armed watchmen, exposed statues and red and blue lanterns in the Venetian style lighted at intervals in the clumps of trees—and also, great isolation.

Prince Forsiani was walking in the shadows; a gust of breeze passed through the leaves; he darted a glance around him; he was certainly quite alone.

"Finally!" he said, with a sigh. "Let's leave that."

At the crossroads of the wide pathway, a lantern placed on a heap of stones illuminated his face.

A few moments later, a new arrival, whose capacious black velvet cloak was lustrous with reflected lamplight, approached him. When the other was before the prince he removed his toque and bowed to him with a graceful gesture.

"Good evening, my dear Wilhelm," said the prince, extending his hand to him.

His parted cloak allowed the sight of rich garments and the fine proportions to his tall stature. Sashes shone over his breast, attached to his sword-belt. His noble and proud face, whose gravity was heightened by the symptoms of approaching old age, seemed imprinted with melancholy.

As for Wilhelm, he was a splendid young man with long curly black hair, an expression of mildness and insouciance, a pale complexion and beautiful eyes.

"Good evening, Milord," he said. "Pardon me for not being the first at the rendezvous; I went astray on the way, owing to my quality as a stranger."

"Your arm."

They linked arms in the middle of the pathway.

"Has our beautiful Gemma spoken to you about the person to whom I shall introduce you in an hour?" Forsiani continued.

"The Duchess of Esperia has told me that only Your Highness . . ."

"Good. But let's see; after what you've heard, what idea have you formed on that subject?"

"Of Marchesa Tullia Fabriana?"

"Yes," said the prince.

The young man hesitated, and replied: "I imagine a young woman whose actions and words command respect, but who, however, leaves an unsatisfying afterthought."

"Ah!" said the prince; and he gazed at Wilhelm thoughtfully for some time. There was a demi-obscurity of blue shadows; the two strollers could see one another perfectly under the trees.

"My dear child," he said, "You've arrived from your manor in Germany; you're seventeen years old; you know a great deal, and old Walter is a teacher of genius. You're alone in the world. Your name is Count Karl-Wilhelm-Ethelbert of Strally-d'Anthas; you descend from the Strally-d'Anthas of Hungary via your father, and the Tiepolis of Venice via your mother—two princes and a doge; so much the better. You're rich, as the heir of your grandfather; you're brave, you're strong and as beautiful as one of these Italian evenings, on which beautiful ladies don't disdain to commit a lovely dream.

"You've arrived in the heart of Italy, in Florence, to attempt a fortune of power and glory; you have the good fortune, even more, the protection, of the Duchess of Esperia. You're recommended to me by the memory of your good and saintly mother. In sum, you have only to show yourself to summarize, at an age when the common run of men are invisible, what fifty years of struggle and crushing labor cannot give. You have youth! You can demand anything, perhaps obtain anything. You can acquire it early enough to rise rapidly to the summit of a justified ambition.

"Well, I, who am a prince and don't appear to have much about which to complain in this society you're entering, I would have said to you, if, after twenty words, I had not found in your nature something solid and innate: 'Go back to your manor, marry some virtuous and simple young woman; bless the God who has given you this leisure; love, dream, sing, hunt, sleep, do a little good in your vicinity, and above all don't forget to shake the dust off your boots at the frontier for fear of poisoning your forests, your mountains and your life.

"Do you understand?"

"Are you trying to frighten me, Milord?" said Wilhelm, rather nonplussed by that conclusion "Even admitting that I'm risking my life, I'm alone on the world."

There was a moment of silence.

"And then, one only dies once," added the young man, insouciantly.

"Do you think so?" said the prince. "At your age, words only have a vague meaning; later, when one sees their profundity, the heart feels stupor and disgust. You don't know cold and cruel depravities, envenomed treasons and their thousands of complications, ending in quotidian ennui; envious hateful and smiling amities; perfidious webs in which one loses love and faith, often honor and dignity, without knowing why or how it happened.

"Oh, you're fortunate! Give passions the time to come, and you'll understand. You believe, you whose heart expands with benevolence and generosity, that people will be interested in you? In the world, people are only interested in those they fear, and you'll find, beneath the most attractive exteriors, indifference and malevolence. Remember that you're going to harm many people by the very fact that you're rich, young and noble—which is to say, by virtue of all the qualities that seemingly ought to make people love you. Instead of the sun, we have chandeliers, instead of faces, masks, instead if sentiments, sensation. You expect men, women and young people? Those who deny specters don't know the world. But let's pass on. You're made of resistant cloth; that's sufficient."

The old courtier was speaking in a manner so natural that the young man shuddered slightly.

"Your Highness will deign to admit, at least, that the first two faces I have encountered belie passably the picture you've just painted of them. Isn't that a good augury for the future?"

"Don't thank me, Wilhelm," Forsiani continued. "I knew your mother once—I tell you that again—and if not for your distinction and charming courage, I would love you for her sake."

The prince added: "You're going to be put in the presence of a woman of extraordinary intelligence and exceptional influence. Few people know her; there is little talk about her; I am convinced, however, that she is the most powerful woman in Italy at present. People try to get around her, but she hides her soul and her thought with an inviolable talent. As she possesses the intuition of physiognomies, you see, my child, to a degree that no one else attains, she will define you accurately and rapidly. Be before her what you are: be naïve; be simple. She is above others, so she can still experience a human sentiment. If you have the good fortune to awaken in her a stir of sympathy, amity, benevolence or amour—no matter which—you will only have to allow yourself to be led blindfold and you will arrive wherever you wish. I've spoken to her about you."

"Ah!" said the count.

Forsiani looked at him. "What surprises me," he continued, "is the bright and unaccustomed gaze with which she accompanied her phrase: 'Bring him to me,' and the unusual attention that she appeared to pay to the fact of your recent arrival in Florence. There was something different in the sound of her voice. I didn't know that manner and was astonished by that abrupt interest in a matter of secondary importance. In sum, I believe that she desires to see you, and it's a rare merit that she's giving you in that."

"Is it possible?" cried Wilhelm, radiantly.

He had a question on his lips, but he dared not interrupt the prince, who divined it.

"She appears to be twenty-four," Forsiani added, "she is actually twenty-six or twenty-seven. It's difficult to imagine a woman more beautiful. She's blonde, with a complexion as white as that statue, and dark eyes of an admirable expression. You'll be charmed by the marvelous distinction of her features and the extraordinary softness of her voice. The simplicity of her speech will seem very natural to you at first, and very casual; then, on looking closer, you'll see what measured exactitude and self-assurance she retains in the strength of that apparent carelessness. It's the greatest human superiority, my dear friend; intelligence constantly in control of itself, always masters others.

"She has never been known or suspected to have any lovers. One remarkable thing is that, in spite of the passions she must excite, in spite of her intact reputation, her superior soul, her great fortune, her nobility and her beauty, no one has asked for her in marriage, I believe, except for one—who was very politely refused, it's true. You know him; it's the English gentleman who was playing against you yesterday evening."

"Lord Seymour?" exclaimed Wilhelm.

"Lower your voice, my dear Wilhelm; there's no need for anyone to overhear us. Yes, Lord Henry Seymour. What do you think of that gentleman?"

"I feel less attracted toward him than anyone else, I confess," said the count, naïvely.

"But it's to him that you addressed yourself first," continued the prince. "Yes, I believe in certain fatalities . . . If you're welcomed in the home of Marchesa Fabriana, beware of Lord Henry; he's a man of cunning and violent projects, in spite of his coldness. He has various contained fashions that have informed me further regarding his character. I regret not being able to abandon, in order to watch over you, the mission with which I'm charged, for I love you like my own child and I fear that something bad might happen to you. It's fortunate that Duchess Gemma has given you her good graces; she's a woman of experience, who will warn me. Here, in any case, is the address of a man sufficiently unknown, who can inform you as to the value of a well-handled sword. Introduce yourself to him on my part."

They stopped under the foliage, illuminated by a lantern. The prince traced two lines, tentatively, on his knee. Wilhelm put the piece of paper in his doublet. If it had been given to anyone to be able to read his soul at that moment, he would have seen the most profound astonishment provoked by Forsiani's words and actions.

"Ah! That's because you've seen me unmasked, my dear Count," said the prince, who understood, laughing. "Let's walk this way for a while," he added, "it's nine-thirty and I still have a good deal to tell you."

"How good you are to me, Milord! How I love you!"

"Thank you," said the prince. "I confess, dear child, that I wouldn't be sorry to find a little sincere amity before dying."

And they resumed their stroll under the trees.

Chapter III

A Nocturnal Stroll

"THIS, in brief, is the story of the rather strange nobility of Fabriana," the prince continued. "It's as
well that you know it. Tullia Fabriana descends, on the
distaff side, from the Venetian Fabrianis, whose name
the family took, and on the male side from the Viscontis
of Pisa, who are not linked by any parentage to those
of Milan. The principal chiefs of that noble house were
two young adventurers, Lamberto and Ubaldo Visconti,
who, one fine day in the year of grace 1192, I believe,
bored with living unknown, came with a handful of
peasants to conquer almost all of south Sardinia.[1]

"It's scarcely more difficult than that for energetic
men in any century. There's even a little story in that
subject. Pope Innocent III, pretexting rights delegated
by no one knows whom, either claiming the conquest

---

1 Lamberto and Ubaldo Visconti were, indeed, captains who made
their mark in military adventures in the early thirteenth century and
Lamberto did found a dynasty that ruled Sardinia, but the account
of hypothetical earlier adventures given here is largely fictitious,

and the authority of two subjects about whom he was much less preoccupied the day before, or harshly and simply making that admirable feat of arms a question of scribes and custom duties, demanded the remission of the conquered towns. There was hesitation. In short, the Viscontis refused. The impetuous pontiff excommunicated them.

"Before that fact, in such an epoch, there were only two ways to go: to submit, or to feign a submission, and, in the latter case, return to Italy trailing their petty troops, disembark at different points, march by night, surround the Very Holy Father, take him by surprise, set fire to the Vatican and end up instituting and confirming themselves, by their own entitlement, plenipotentiaries of the rights of the Church and sovereigns of Italy.

"They would not have been risking anything, already having been banished from human dignity by the bull that weighed upon them. Incur captivity, torture and death? Such soldiers have no intention of letting themselves be taken alive! Raise against them half a dozen kings and the clergy of Europe? Perhaps. On looking closely at the history of those times, one wonders whether they would not have encountered more partisans than enemies. But it is difficult to dare, even for the Henri IVs of Germany.

"Lamberto Visconti submitted—these swordsmen! It was only Gregory VI who lifted the excommunication. An ingenious contract was stipulated. Lamberto married a certain Gherardesca, a near relative of the Pope. Ubaldo, rebellious, created a judicature of seven towns out there in Sardinia, and governed. That created two parties, of which the hearth came to be centralized in Florence, and that is the little-known origin of the contest of the Ghibellines and the Guelphs.

"I've told you that story not only to enable you to appreciate the excellence of Tullia Fabriana's nobility, but also to indicate to you, in passing, how many seemingly reckless actions become *coups d'état* and end up being accepted, enchaining and mingling in a manner both simple and bizarre with the general fluctuation.

"I beg you, my dear child, not to conclude from this that I'm not a Christian. These circumstances do not touch the eternal dogma in any fashion, and without even wanting to mention the likes of Alexander VI, Urban V, Julius II and the rest, there are, as you know, many less tolerable in world history. A belief that, in spite of so many scandals, subsists for so many centuries and finds martyrs every day, proves by that fact that it signifies something; and that band of crooks, far from serving as arguments against it, demonstrates the solidity of its throne. I'm recounting impartially, that's all."

"Thank you, Milord," said Wilhelm.

Was there a more singular Christian than the ambassador?

"In addition to those men of war," Prince Forsiani continued, "our Marchesa counts a good number of illustrious names inscribed in the golden book of Venice and the annals of Italy. She leads a solitary life, receives rarely and sometimes travels. She is alone in the world, like you, but for seven or eight years. Her mother was a very simple woman. While she was alive, I saw them sympathetic to one another. The Marchesa never talks about her, nor about her family; she seems, surprisingly enough, to have forgotten both of them. I know that she gives away a considerable part of her fortune in alms; this is generosity; but perhaps there are less ordinary secrets in her life. I don't believe her to be incapable of great actions. May she, as I hope, take you in amity!"

Quarter to ten chimed at the Pitti Palace.

"Now Wilhelm, I'll give you some items of practical advice; take them as the words of a man who loves you, and for whom many things are finished. I'm leaving in five or six hours; I'm at an age when one doubts that one will see again those whom one is quitting. It's necessary that I put you on your guard somewhat against existence. In brief, this is the way to go if you want to arrive high quickly, whatever happens, and if you want to remain worthy of your ambition.

"You don't resemble the majority of young men of your age, otherwise I'd begin by saying to you: 'My dear Count, I have no advice to give you. If you retain enough health and conscience, a year from now, to reflect on yourself and I have the pleasure of seeing you again, I'll have something to teach you. You'll have acquired, in that year of distractions, a theoretical view of existence, but as the sense of verity will have been completely shaken in your heart, I wish you courage. For now, good luck and goodbye,'

"I would have spoken like that; but you, my child, I can advise. Oh, I understand youth, and I can't be sorry that it relaxes sometimes and lets itself go to the enjoyment of its twenty years. One is only twenty for a few days. But the important life is that in which the actions don't trouble our dignity, reinforce the sublime sentiments of our hopes, give us interior serenity and authorize us thereby to have confidence in death. It is about that existence of difficult struggles that I want to talk to you.

"You're going to be dealing with men who almost all think themselves capable of changing the world, each of whom thinks more of himself than his neighbor— which, seen at close range, constitutes the clearest evidence of apparent universal equality. If someone finds you young, say nothing, but weigh the social and practical resultant of the man who finds you young and you'll be astonished to see that it's almost always negligible or insignificant.

"Don't listen to all those people who view things from a height; they see them from so high up that they end up no longer distinguishing anything. Never allow yourself to be dazzled by their affirmations. Decompose in thought each of the terms they enunciate, and most of the time you'll find the ensemble stupid or naïve. Often, you'll hear a man say something profound, and ramble a minute after. Anyone can say profound things! It's combining them that's difficult. The man who can do that is a man.

"If you have an interest in a discussion with serious consequences—never take part in others—in which someone or other talks at length against your ideas, bring up a petty disagreeable detail of his conduct or private life; have no fear of entering into it, unceremoniously, as a master, and make unexpected spectacles seen by dilating that annoying detail; one can fell lions with similar trivia. I regret not being able to make that experiment before you, in order to show you what results from it, but being only a question of tact, you ought to comprehend the thousand gracious manners with which it is surrounded.

"If you intend your advice to be accepted, know this: to be right is to be *more* right. At what goal are you aiming? To bring someone to your own views? Never commence, then, by wounding the other with an absolute denigration of his opinion. Say what he says and if you have something beyond it, make him see it; he will come to it of his own accord; but he would die in the breach rather than let go of the idea that you are wrong if you begin by denying what he says. Never get carried away, in any circumstance! If you are no longer master of your own speech, how will you be of the speech of others?"

Wilhelm listened to all these simple things with great attention. Night was advancing in the sky. The prince continued placidly:

"And then, Count, it's necessary to have charity, you see; charity is respect for one's neighbor. By respecting a man, even the most fallen, you can make him your dog if you wish, so much is the sentiment of nobility elevated in the man. To arrive at respecting any man who has acted in a revolting manner, it is only necessary to pose this dilemma: either the man had a reason for committing such a wretched action, or he did not. If he did not, he's a madman whom it's necessary to pity and not to judge or despise; if he did, it's evident that I, endowed with reason like him, and similarly human, if I had been placed in the same conditions and circumstances as him and impelled by the same motives as him, would have done as he did, since he did it for a reason.

"Never judge a man, then, and always respect him, no matter what he has done. Only judge the action, because it is necessary to decree something in order to live sociably, and pass on. Trying to discover motives is impossible and, in any case, they are futile and unfathomable; it's another world than ours. It's necessary to respect the man because one is human, and ought to respect humanity in the other.

"As for the other's ideas, that's another matter. It's unnecessary to cling to the admiration or indifference of people whose criticism or esteem obeys the same motives as the wave that comes and goes. Does that count? Should one occupy oneself with it? It's the dust of the road; it's the passing wind. Let those people speak who only recite for almost all their lives, imagining that no one can have thought differently from themselves. If you knew how little it is, in sum! If you knew how ridiculous, pitiful and malign they are!

"Look, yesterday's soirée seemed quite agreeable to you, your introduction to the nuncio quite simple, the generosity of the Duchess of Esperia and my amity quite natural? You have no idea what those events provoked of vile thoughts, abject reasoning and infamous insinuations! You can't imagine what translations I read, beneath the masks of serenity, in those little smiles crawling like vipers over the lips of those handsome young men and charming women. It would have been sufficient for me to pronounce two or three elegant and measured words to make numerous fans quiver and bring silence and pallor to the insouciant stupidity of many of those faces, but it's necessary to forgive those who know not what they do. You'll see those gallants who permit themselves to mock a noble action, believing that they can define it because they perceive one aspect of it from their own stature! They are attentive to women and have courage before danger, but no soul in confrontation with Heaven, conscience and creation: beautiful manners, perfumed gloves and fine moustaches—a heap of bones, all that!

"Take two words of cold poverty to evaluate those fine dignities! How you see them, calculating and committing incredible, nameless base actions—in order to live? Not at all! They are acting out of ennui, weakness and cowardice, in order to procure the pettiest pleasure. I've seen that so many times! A man of common sense, who is alone, with two good arms and courage, cannot fail to live anywhere, but those philosophers esteem that labor is a weakness. Good for them!

"Do you believe that a hundred of those men of taste are worth as much as a peasant who loves a worthy wife, beats her from time to time, raises his family, works the land and deigns to pray to God? That, however, is society in all its splendor, my dear Wilhelm! Oh well, don't despise it. You can't understand the forces of impulsion graduated toward infamy, the mechanisms of baseness and crime, the insensible pressures that lead there. They are abysms! Lament and respect, in spite of everything, if you want to see something in life . . . more than life!

"In a word, have the charity that I mentioned to you a little while ago. You've understood me, haven't you?"

"Oh, my dear Prince, that puts a chill in the heart!"

"Yes, it is rather cold, but one gets used to it. Some advice for you, now. I know that you're modest, I'm sure that you always will be, in speech at least, because modesty is logical pride. You're rich—so much the better—but never run up debts, even if it's a matter of a throne, for the simple reason that you might die before acquitting yourself, that it might be forgotten, and if you want to be sure of yourself, its important that you're ready to die at any moment, such as fate determines, without owing anything to anyone. That's true dignity.

"Never hesitate; always act when the occasion arises; do no matter what, but do something; all actions are equal in value, very nearly, for the man who is able to find the juncture and extract its real value—which is to say, for the man who can discover the greatest number of possible relationships of some event with the absolute goal of his existence; groping natures never arrive at anything solid; thus, always act before the occasion by deploying all the resources of your presence of mind.

"Never link yourself to anyone to the point of delivering yourself in speech—never! That doesn't lead to anything worthwhile, and it diminishes the will and respect for one's goal, even if your friend is the ideal of friends. Believe, my dear child, that I have required frequent experiments in order for me to presume that. Talk about indifferent things, let others speak, and have no fear of rendering service to anyone, even if you have been afflicted twenty times over for having done it. If you receive advances—and you will—have courage! Constrain your good heart. Receive them coldly: no confidences or expansions of any sort, or you will be less esteemed tomorrow.

"Oh, that's hard at your age, I know; but it's necessary to choose between an obscure and a glorious destiny, and once the choice is made, to maintain an iron will with regard to what an instant's forgetfulness might bite. A man who risks a future for the amusement of a minute's talk doubts himself at that moment, and, in consequence, does not deserve to succeed.

"The world belongs to a man sufficiently concentrated and sufficiently master of his will and his thought, to act without responding to other men with anything but 'yes' or 'no,' indifferently, throughout his life.

"Have no fear of making enemies, if necessary— enemies that bear grudges! They're often more useful than friends. Friends are often sufficiently occupied with themselves; enemies occupy themselves with you and prepare for you what you need to exercise your faculty for overcoming obstacles. Obstacles are as necessary as bread. Does not the man who wants to vanquish need enemies?

"When you speak, continue neither to smile nor raise your eyebrows, in order to maintain as much immobility as possible in the face . . . if I say this to you, it's because I want you to be perfect, my child . . . be grave and indifferent. To pronounce the strongest, most humane and most profound words that seem to want to impose themselves would be to alienate the mind of society maladroitly: one would appear to want to appear, which is fatal."

Wilhelm was mute with attention.

"What I'm saying to you appears to you at present to be very simple, doesn't it? You can't know how much this advice has cost me. But know, Wilhelm, that the most renowned sages, prophets or demigods, have only overturned the world with simplicities of this sort, because they are almost the only exactitudes of life, and—a truly mysterious thing—one only returns to them after having made a tour of existence.

"Open the few books left by the great men, the likes of the Bible, the Koran, and so on, and you will find a surprising ingenuousness therein, things that you have said to yourself a hundred times: 'Love one another! Do no harm to others, etc. 'There is no other God than God,' etc., and a thousand variants. Then you wonder how, with phrases of that naïvety, phrases written in the depths of all consciences, it has been possible to transfigure human societies and establish oneself as a prophet or a god.

"The thinker does not stop at those words; he finds them too simple; he often forgets that faith is not a conviction but an action: the act of assimilating the most divine evidence possible, each in the moment and in accordance with the sphere in which he finds himself.

"Oh, if you knew how much terrible and fast-moving power a seemingly banal word contains. Look: five continents make up the world; there are more than a billion human beings therein, all very knowledgeable in their métiers, in their detail; by whom is all that managed, stirred and governed? By a hundred individuals of an intelligence that is almost always quite ordinary. The majority of them amuse themselves royally, I assure you;

it is only their milieux of grandeur that elevate them; they know intimately, moreover, that they are getting it cheaply. One of then—this is modern history—after having had more than eighty million people . . . do you hear that figure? . . . for his share, at nineteen years of age, after having been the suzerain of a dozen kings, after having won victory after victory, after having been greater than Caesar, and after having possessed the purple, ermines, scepters and imperial triple crowns, went to make supper for two or three monks in the quality of a lay brother and wash their various household utensils. Can you see that warrior, that great politician, that fine legislator, that master of Europe, retaining his coarse habit and gravely accomplishing his labor? So you think that he did not require as much intelligence then as he once did to conquer Tiemcen, Rome, Pavia, Mühlberg, etc., and that it was not worth as much as the causes of Suetonius' twelve irritated men?"[1]

"Oh, that's true!" murmured Wilhelm. "It's frightening!"

"Because you see the word *Charles* and the word *Quint*, and you lose sight of the man beneath those two prestigious words. That surpasses you. It's necessary never to forget the cadaver. That individual, like other emperors and kings, only represents the consequence of a word pronounced centuries ago. You see what a word can produce. Someone opens his mouth and articulates some idea applicable to a general fact; that idea is decomposed, absorbed and assimilated in a billion

---

1 A slighting reference to Suetonius' study *De vita Caesarum*, generally known as *The Twelve Caesars*.

different ways by a billion different brains, which have a billion different ways of understanding words and seeing things. Everyone admires it because everyone sees in it his own idea—often emitted at random—and each can apply it usefully in accordance with the degree of his intelligence, relative to the functions he exercises.

"In brief, with a common accord, the man and his idea end up becoming miraculous, simply because opening the mouth, the principle of the general event, is already a miracle. The simpler the idea is, the more one can dispense with intelligence, and the more meditation its produces in consequence, and the more people are found to come along centuries later and heap their own sum of ingenuousness upon it. That's all history is, neither more nor less, my dear Count, believe me.

"You'll admit, however, that there would be no reason for the great dream to be accomplished if there were no law or goal, if there were nothing underneath it all—in sum that it would be a very mysterious stupidity! Don't conclude from it, therefore, scorn for humankind, but the power of human speech."

The moon was shining through the trees. Its radiance, through the foliage, illuminated the two strollers. Wilhelm could have believed that he was in Germany. He remained silent; he was listening.

"As for women," added Prince Forsiani, "I believe it to be unnecessary to give you the midday sun with regard to a woman of the evening, a gracious individual who emerged from the dormitory at eighteen and who counts eight or ten years of services: keep your dreams! They're better than the reality. Only, as I don't want you,

44

definitively, to be taken by surprise, I want to put you in the presence of a genuine woman, a woman whom I esteem and admire.

"Yes, I confess to you that if I were not living with the memory of another, a memory that fills my soul—and which is sufficient for me—Marchesa Tullia would appear to me to be the only woman possible for a superior man. The more I think about it, the more I find that there is something in her that is very elevated; and if you touch her, if she wants to admit you into her intimacy, she will enable you to live, in the full meaning of the word. I've always seen what she is; I've known her for ten years, having been closely linked with her father, Duke Belial Fabriano, who died poisoned in the home of one of his friends, because of hatreds dating from a long way back in the family.

"In that epoch she was very nearly what she is now. At first sight, she's a woman of the world, perfectly elegant. On looking closer, and paying attention—for she never delivers herself, and it's necessary to seize a nuance to sense it—all her charming advantages are deformed in proportions so indefinable that I shall abstain from qualifying the value of her intelligence. You'll probably be surprised by that nature, and by a phenomenon as striking that her conversation presents, which is the change of aspect that the most ordinary actions seem to take on when she speaks.

"What I'm going to tell you is perhaps hazarded by dint of being grave and abnormal, but she sometimes says things that awaken unknown . . . I don't want to say *forgotten* . . . impressions in the mind. Anyway, you'll

45

see. Human sentiments, my dear child, for that strange person, are reduced to a sure and profound mechanism that she operates, smiling, with as much precision and fatality as the moves in a game of chess. Once, she gave me some advice; I followed it, and it avoided a war. It was definitely remarkably clever, and I still wonder how she was even able to offer it to me. In sum, I've never understood better than this evening that I know nothing very precise about the subject of Tullia Fabriana . . .

"Truly, when one thinks about it, there's something tenebrous about that woman," the prince added, as if talking to himself. There was a moment of silence thereafter. "But there's ten o'clock chiming; come. Don't judge her on what she says to you this evening—the mask, you know. Do you have horses nearby?"

"Yes, Milord," said Wilhelm, with the air of a man awakened with a start

"Good; otherwise I would have had to take you in my carriage. Give me your hand, again. Remember in the time and place what I've said to you, and forgive what there is that's a little . . . supreme . . . in my advice in favor of my tenderness for you."

"Milord, I shall never forget this evening," said the young man. "I'm so moved that I don't know how to speak, and to thank you with all my heart."

"Dear child!" said the prince, with a long pensive gaze, and he murmured very softly, in the shadow: "Oh the beautiful nocturnal stars of youth! Amours! Lost enthusiasms! Here's the spring, while leaves are falling around the others. Poor human hope!" Aloud, he said: "Let's go—to horse!"

"Christian!" called the Count of Strally.

"Yes, sir?" said a newcomer, running toward the two strollers. It was an old domestic.

Prince Forliani scanned him with a glance and appeared content with the ensemble.

"Our horses, quickly!" said the count.

A few minutes later, they stopped outside one of the grand palaces near the Arno; the doors opened as before people expected, and they climbed the steps of the immense marble staircase . . .

Chapter IV

First Sight of Tullia Fabriana

The solitary is surrounded by everything that magnifies his reason, raises him above himself and gives him the sentiment of immortality, whereas the man of the world only lives an ephemeral life. The solitary finds in his retreat a compensation for all the vain pleasures of which he deprives himself, whereas the man of the world thinks that all is lost if he fails to appear at an assembly or neglects a spectacle.

(Zimmermann, *Solitude*.)[1]

IF the woman whose allures preoccupied Prince Forsiani had been dead at the moment when he was talking about her to Count d'Anthas, this is what it would have been possible for an observer to summarize on the subject of the existence of that person, if he

---

1 The philosopher Johann von Zimmermann (1728-1795) published the first version of *Über die Einsamkeit* [On Solitude] in 1756. It was translated into French as *La Solitude* in 1845.

desired to consecrate a biographical notice to universal usage:

Tullia Fabriana was one of those great minds, superior individuals, constituted by the precocious experience of events, meditation and the world.

Such people, before being perceived and before being carried away by the current, soon take account of existence and, in consequence, have the time to furl their great wings in order not to overshadow others. By virtue of reconstructing and fathoming events, she found action distasteful.

Certainly, the renown of glorious women must have darkened her lovely brow more than once, but on reflection, satisfied with the scarcely dependent status in which her birth had placed her, she had made the decision to live in an egotistical concentration. Isolation sufficed for her. She had succeeded, gradually, without apparent resolution, in veiling her veritable life as hermetically as possible.

Isolation! The special favor of destiny! A privilege whose prescription is always without appeal. To whom, today, is the power to isolate themselves given? Persons of a rich position or elevated rank acquire that supreme advantage with all the more difficulty because the quotidian relationships of their existence make them the focal point and pivot of thousands of individual desires and interests that gather together, enchaining and attenuating, all the way to the topmost steps of the social hierarchy. Humanity gathers around a single individual and surrounds them with a vigilance and obstinacy motivated by the order of things.

Considering the industrial threads of all centuries and all lands, which label and subdivide one another to the point where the relativity can no longer be distinguished, whereas those stripped down to the perfect and normal state only loom up everywhere with a cortege of sadness, one is less astonished that the movement of one alone determines that incalculable series of profits and prejudices. As, on the other hand, those profits and prejudices are sometimes of vital importance for those involved, people given to meditation, travail and silence experience great difficulty in avoiding the insignificant dissipations of speech and the diffusions of self that contact with others never fails to entail.

Thanks to the miraculous equilibrium of almost all the societies of the Occident, an equilibrium combined from the resultant of an equal number of organizing forces and contrary forces, the movement of each one, from the beggar to the prince and from the cradle to the grave can remain foreseen, defined and regulated by the various European legal codes. Such a reflection will suffice to demonstrate the impossibility of a durable isolation in any European city. It is necessary to live with one's fellows, and that immense law, like the net of a retiarius, wraps around people precisely by reason of the efforts they make to disengage themselves. No one can extract themselves from that infinite liaison. It goes as far as to render individuals a solidarity with one another without them being aware of it, which would even astonish a Christian, if the Christian did not always retain, in the depths of his thought, presentiments of a solution for any problem, which is not to flinch more frequently, except because of one's neighbor's movements, and not to fall, at any time, except by virtue of the consequences of lesser actions, and thanks to the imperfection of codes, under the scourge of correctional jurisdiction.

It is noticeable, moreover, that few people escape throughout life some affliction of the law. That affirmation might be surprising, but even in the most retired and purest existence, it is perhaps not impossible, with the aid of a scrupulous examination, to discover at least one little legal stain, a trace of judiciary entanglement. One is not free to distance oneself from universal interests, no matter how indifferent one might be, simply because one is a part of universal interests. Do not the virtue, dignity and domestic wellbeing of every individual depend on something trivial, a detail or a gesture? Where is the honest citizen sure enough of his temperament to dare to affirm that, for example, the excess of a glass of wine, risked in the most attenuating circumstances, could not have consequences that would take him to a convict prison?

The Christian might say that that tends to prove that our real liberty, dignity and wellbeing are not of this world; in the meantime, only they are really free and really alone to whom it is given to cross, from summit to summit, the hierarchy of ideas, because they offer scarcely any purchase to the violent desires and scarcely worry about the woes or joys that the earth presents to them. They are not preoccupied beyond measure with living or dying; everything is defined tranquilly in their eyes; they do as much good, in the simplest meaning of the term, as it is given to them to be able to do, and are unable either to hate or condemn. Their eyes fixed on the idea, it is permitted to them to judge, because they love and they pardon. They draw from the infinity of that interior expansion the principle of immortality.

If they deign to take part in the universal agitation, as soldiers or thinkers, to the former, the golden throne of the law, the principle of the brutal forces the earth, and to the latter the diamond scepter of speech, the principle of the motive forces of society. But also, a few profound wounds hide the radiance of their glory. Can Sisyphus be imagined without the rock, Socrates without the hemlock, or Prometheus without the vulture? The egotistical disgust and permanent indifference of other men absorbed by detail are fundamentally nothing but a muffled envy directed against them; by excavating the motives of that sentiment one ends up understanding it and granting it mercy; is it any less sad for that? And are its consequences for the heroic man any less deadly? Fortunate, therefore are those who can, while soaring, hide their grandeur. They are not crucified.

Tullia Fabriana held herself at a distance, having everything to give and little to receive in the banal commerce of society. Unable to break with it entirely, by virtue of her essentially social position, she only allowed to be seen that which it was strictly impossible for her to hide. The rest of the time she lived alone and in her thought. In conversation she was a pneumatic nature by which the minds of others were rapidly turned round, understood and evaluated without their knowledge, by virtue of an almost infallible calculation of systematized trivia. As she knew how to say everything, she knew how to impede when anyone ventured a little into her consciousness.

The secret of that skill consisted in the ungraspable difficulty of the transitions that she allowed to be experienced between a given point of departure and a more expansive current of ideas: a sure method of never being obliged to offend anyone and to retain an external urbanity while conserving solitary indifference internally. Her age seconded her somewhat, moreover, in successes of that sort. The absence of indecision in the gaze and the bearing, a quality that generally specialized women of that seasoning, was presented so magnetically in her beauty that the mere sight of her froze insipidities on the lips. She had even arrived at such a degree of interior strength that the half-mocking, half-paternal smile that old gentlemen, for instance, permit themselves mildly with regard to women—the charm and grace of which suddenly brighten their faces—was always troubled before the very simple and virile dignity of the mysterious woman.

Few beings are endowed with a fascinating fluid of which eloquent and cold minds cannot take account and to which, however, they are submissive in an insurmountable, inexplicable and sudden manner. The vulgar, who laugh and pass on, do not believe in that superiority; a little suffices for them. That empire is only challenged in the rare instances when it finds itself in contact with one of the beings who exercise it. The vulgar person is similar to a sly country bumpkin who mocks an electric battery but changes his face as soon as he touches the wire. It is true that their astonishment only lasts for an hour and is concluded by some skeptical or indifferent remark. The vulgar knew nothing of Tullia Fabriana but her name, and that name was surrounded by dignity and respect. A sentiment of consideration and profound sympathy emanated from her, which, imposing itself naturally on all those who approached her, was accepted without any shock or argument.

Life is a choice to be made; it is only a matter of wanting to grow in oneself in order to feel alive. Everything, for us, is in the will! Some people, under the pretext that one must die, that all is vanity, that their classic illusions are lost, and other fictions, hold to those glimpses of themselves and, refusing elevated impressions, drag the cannonball of an existence devoid of an ideal. They are the first dupes of their lack of foresight. Such a positivism approaches instinct. One becomes insignificant for oneself, and that drawing-room armor cannot hold against two hours of practical struggle. It is necessary not to be astonished by anything, according to their motto: the man who is not astonished by anything ought to begin by finding himself astonishing.

If they were only sincere, those philosophers! But the first milieu that comes along is sufficient to distract them and strike them with contradiction. If they even became better! But, impotent to suffer alone, they only take pleasure in chilling the placid hopes of others. Every speech contains a force, and as they speak without paying much heed to the scandal contained in their words, that scandal, being something, progresses through crowds and across centuries. Thus, the discourse of one unhappy person of intermittent conviction, the phrase of a man who might perhaps have admired the next day, depending on the humor of the moment, what he charged with derision the day before, can go forth to destroy the meditation of a number of the condemned who hear it and who, taking themselves seriously, take the word of the false brother seriously. Then the propaganda recommences, more loudly. A sad origin of doubt.

In sum, does the contraction of the venerable rictuses of a million hilarious worthies who, under the pretext of lost illusions, spend the major part of their careers expressly in seeing nothing anywhere, constitute a sufficient fact of presence for them to be awarded a valid right of decision in profound questions? Have they really formulated, by that arbitrary grimace, the last expression of philosophy? It is at least dubious, since philosophy understands them, in the depths of its inferior deductions, and, by their own admission, they extract their greatest glory from what they do not understand.

Therefore, since they are as if they were not, for want of a little soul and good will, the thinker ought not to pay any heed to them. They are like those accursed lakes, those dead waters, whose vapors kill the birds of the air if their wings are not powerful enough to cross them at a stroke.

It is rather difficult to perceive them; generally, confirmed and ripened cynics are encountered in the elevated castes whose members, rightly or wrongly, lead joyful lives somewhat at the expense of universal labor. That will cease when the scythe of justice reaches as far as them; but it is the case at present, and almost always has been. Those people have no other value than the impulsion they provide by means of the dispensation of their fortune. It is therefore necessary to show them a certain deference because of that force, with which social organization invests them gratuitously, and with which they can do harm. Inevitable everyday relations oblige elevated souls to associate with those souls who have remained on the road, under the penalty of seeing the simplest action become the target of all sorts of impudent commentary; society, lending its grandeurs to pettiness, does not believe in the disinterest of genius.

It is doubtless for that reason that Tullia Fabriana sometimes received the brilliant flux of that society, of which she could not prohibit the sight, but whose collective consciousness stopped before hers like the sea before a rock.

Thus, in the drawing rooms of her palace on the Arno, Tuscan princes were encountered, old diplomats with faces always veiled by a conventional worry, handsome Florentine cavaliers, attachés from various legations whose somber costumes were heightened by ribbons, precious stones or various other marks of distinction, young heiresses of the most illustrious families in Italy and the great artists of the time. The palace emerged from its shadow on the illuminated quays; the waves, speckled with gleams, were stirred by the embalmed nocturnal breezes; the gardens that bordered the exterior peristyles sparkled in their foliage, and insouciant splendid couples wandered over the lawns and under the dense orange-trees.

On those evenings the beautiful sovereign was humanized and transfigured; she found a word of welcome for each of her guests; her Oriental beauty was framed by that resplendent entourage and had a particularity that was sympathetic even for women in whom it did not excite any malevolent afterthought of envy or hatred. When the fête was over, people talked about her all over Florence for some time, but only as a free and placid aristocrat determined to maintain her placid liberty nobly.

Chapter V

Transfiguration

> She walks in beauty, like the night
> Of cloudless climes and starry skies.
> (Lord Byron, *Hebrew Melodies.*)

A N ordinary physiognomist could doubtless have succeeded in combining those data on the subject of Marchesa Tullia Fabrana, and it would have been difficult to define her in a more precise manner.

Without being of superior flight in that regard, one can seize with facility the predispositions and the instincts of a soul in accordance with the lines in repose of its visible form, in the sound of the voice, the mannerisms, the expressions, etc.—but to read an obsession through the folds of the exterior, to know the true nature and the dominant impulsion of an Intelligence, to divine, positively, the great motive hidden in al the precautions of genius, is no longer the mechanism of intuition; it depends on the will-power of the subject.

Of what value were the observations of Zeno regarding the impressed mask of Socrates? None, in fact. The clairvoyance of the physiognomist can do nothing past a certain limit imposed on it by facial fatality. The most powerful analyzer dealing, for example, with a human exception, can fall falsely upon a detail and mistake it for the basis of the ensemble, when it is only the temporary result of the milieu in which he is studying him. Those sorts of schools are not rare among the most expert. The science of the human face being all presentiment in its principles, to reconstruct the life of a person after a rapid examination of his features, to see, one after another, his aptitudes and preferred passions, to determine his future possibilities according to the probable results of some crease of the mouth while smiling, some accentuation of the wrinkles, or some appreciation of both those data, anyone can do more or less exactly, unawares. For observers there are nuances that others, less sensitive, do not perceive; they render accounts of their neighbors in an almost reliable fashion. Nothing escapes men endowed with intuitive incarnation. They put themselves into the other and look at themselves there as if in a mirror; they listen impersonally to their speech and judge accurately, in consequence, when they speak.

One final word on that subject. The simple observer is able to draw an excellent result for himself when the occasion presents itself; that is what the majority of respectable mortals, only ever seeing a result, without appreciating the cause, call "being lucky"—as if one could continue being lucky for a long time and with impunity in the midst of a group of societies regulated by thirty-two codes! To grasp the opportunity coolly and to render what one can give is already marching in conformity with the logic of fate, and it is remarkable. But the people about whom we want to talk, people endowed with intuitive incarnation, are capable of creating the opportunity, of giving birth to the milieu from which they would like to profit. The combined forces of amour and gold would positively fall before those redoubtable and rare individuals, if they wanted to succeed in some such project; but ordinarily, they truly do not care about anything. That power draws disgust. If destiny does not make them advances they end up, for the most part, in embarrassment and saddened by their grandeur. They await death naïvely, those princes of the human race. More than that, their very strength is harmful, principally when the necessary is in question for them. Then their calm sometimes weakens and they operate such prodigies of reconstruction that they surpass the goal a hundred times over, entangled in their sublime wings, and, in fact, are deflected by the stupidity of the living.

If, therefore, one of them had crossed the path of Tullia Fabriana it would have been a rather sharp astonishment for him to sense that he was incapable of understanding her. Not one contradiction in that face! A mild gaze, even and assured, a delectably pure harmony of lines; in sum, nothing would have justified for him the troubled intuition, the muted warning of the unknown, that he experienced before her.

Nothing: the woman's forms were sculpted of their own accord on the marble of that virgin body; grace undulated in her movements; strength ran in her healthy and pure limbs, beauty enveloped her entirely with its royal mantle, but no door opened to her thought, no vestiges of existence . . .

However, if it had been given to that man to consider several times, deploying his greatest attention, those calm dark eyes in which the will shone with its eternal light, they would suddenly have seemed as profound to him as the sky!

Around her, something attractive, unusual and grave would have vibrated subsequently for him. An imperious sympathy emerged from that woman, and it was not because she was beautiful. But what ought to remain invisible remained invisible. And even if Tullia Fabriana had not refused any indication of her veritable nature, how could one recognize in a woman placed in an environment of wealth and tranquility, how could one recognize a Genius with vertiginous conceptions, endowed with the energy of a Prometheus or a Lucifer, enlightened in all her depths by a science whose origin would have seemed inexplicable, armed with a sang-froid and a power of dissimulation proof against anything, equipped with a precision of glance and a magisterial logic of action, and, in brief, having incessantly in view the accomplishment of a task of gripping and universal interest; in sum, having resolved something terrible, immense and unknown?

How could such strangeness of Fate be admitted, even in confrontation with the most sovereign evidence?

To surprise her with a combination of words before plunging her into such a circle of ideas, under the light of which one would have liked to submit her to examination; to know what she signified, and to penetrate her? Truly, the execution of such a project would not have been pursued for five minutes in confrontation with her.

As soon as the first instinct of a serious inquisition, and without her casual charm appearing to have undergone the slightest change, a naïve and piercing gaze, like a sword-thrust, would have sufficed to disconcert the chimerical hope of an amateur. It was forbidden to work upon the darkness of that intelligence, for action and thought appeared to have a similar value in her. The most jovial skepticism would have been blunted against her diamond will. Her conversation would not have ceased, for that, to be mocking, light and mild, but betray herself? Not at all. She estimated her soul as something too preferable to the entire universe to allow anyone to glimpse it, and her thoughts as too immutable to be delivered as prey to the discretion of the banal versatility of the first to come along.

Her sublime secret was hidden in her like the ark in the sanctuary of the temple. Vaguely flamboyant, the swords of Levites surrounded her incessantly, in the shadow of days and nights. Woe betide anyone who approached to closely, even to serve her or preserve her; Even if he were a pontiff or a king, his heart would have weakened in his breast, and no one would have known the hand that struck him.

Chapter VI

Study of Childhood

Is the science to which we consecrate our lives
worth what we sacrifice to it? Will we arrive at
a more certain view of human destiny and its
relationship with infinity? Will we know more
clearly the law of the origin of beings, the nature
of consciousness, what life is, and what the personality is?

Renan[1]

On the thirteenth of December 1761, at midnight,
Countess Angelia-Maria de Albornozzo Bruzati,
Princess of Visconti, Duchess of Fabriano, brought into
the world a child who received the name of Tullia.

---

1 The historian Ernest Renan (1823-1892) published his contro-
versial *Vie de Jésus* (tr. as *The Life of Jesus*) in the same year that
Villiers published *Isis*. The quotation does not appear to come from
any of his books published before that date, but might have been
taken from a preliminary exercise of his enquiry into *L'Avenir de
Science* (1869; tr. as *The Future of Science*).

Duke Belial Fabriano might have been fifty-eight years old when he married Countess Angelia. The latter had entered her twentieth year.

The Duke had a Venetian beauty. He took great care of himself and maintained an exemplary cleanliness. His hair was long and silvery; his face, of a habitually grave expression, did not go badly with his Herculean stature. His aristocratic elegance of manners, the witty affability of his attentions, had domesticated the beautiful dove, and she was really more his companion than his daughter. Their union was defined by force of dignity and nuances, in a strangely beautiful fashion. The duke was a man of the world. A part of his life had been spent voyaging; dangerous adventures and difficult hours had tempered his experience, with the result that the gentle Angelia had accepted him less out of duty than contentment, with an amicable and very Christian indifference. It was, in sum, a satisfying sight to see her leaning on his arm. But they lived somewhat in solitude, and rarely saw people.

On the evening when the duchess gave birth to her daughter, she forgot all the repressed demi-aspirations, all the sadness of dreams forever extinct in her soul, and all the scant compensations obtained by religious practices and a tottering devotion!

What a beautiful little girl Tullia was, too! Although her eyes were closed, she already had a kind of smile under the gentle kisses of Duchess Angelia. Finally, she opened her beautiful dark eyes and mirrored them in the exactly similar eyes of her mother.

The ecstasies, memories and celestial joys of a mother! They cannot be analyzed. Eternal nature is hidden in the smile of a young woman who contemplates placidly two soft little lips pressed to her breast and accepting life therefrom.

Several months went by. Already the breath of beauty caressed and impregnated with the ideal the pure lineaments of her form; she was candid, and the glimmer of the soul was as transparent in her as light through an alabaster lamp. Her hair was as tenuous as threads of spider-silk that glisten in summer in the countryside and as silkily silvery as the radiance of stars woven by the nocturnal fays.

She was already walking unaided.

And she grew further. The gardens of the palace, abandoned for a long time, were as vast as deserts; she wandered in the profound pathways, and she got lost without fear in the clumps of wild flowers in the shady thickets of old trees. Her infancy was as silent as a dream, and she grew up in the shadows.

The particularity of Tullia Fabriana's organism—we mean the extraordinary extent of her intellectual aptitudes—developed in that privation and that liberty.

The character of her intelligence was self-determined, and it was by obscure transitions that it attained the immanent proportions in which the self is affirmed for what it is. The nameless hour, the eternal hour in which children cease to gaze vaguely at the sky and the earth, sounded for her in her ninth year. What dreamed confusedly in the eyes of the little girl became a fixed gleam from that moment on; one might have thought that she was experiencing an awareness of herself, awakening in our darkness.

It was at that age that she became pensive. An intense fever of study came to grip her spontaneously, and under the cold assiduity, beneath the calm of her virile and regular constancy, the luminous originality of her nature became manifest. She began to read, to write and to dream . . .

The universe appeared to her clad in a more disquieting aspect than for other girls of her age; but she rarely spoke and did not ask questions. Primitive instincts caused her to flee the companions of amusements that her mother presented to her. However, she withdrew with manners so mild and attentive that she never wounded anyone.

The old duke remarked the cold gaze, the quiet demeanor and surprising predispositions of his daughter. He did not think it appropriate to intervene in such a nature; he sensed that he would have killed it, and that it would have ended by that. As he was a just man in matters of thought and as it appeared that he ought not to die in that manner, he did not refuse to favor the development of that mind.

Thought found in her organs of prehension so vast and so solid, her memory had such a marvelous power that she succeeded in her twelfth year, without becoming fatigued, in mastering several sciences and several languages.

Drawing, sculpture and, above all, great music were her distractions, and although she did not give them much time she showed a remarkable talent therein from day to day.

Apart from the penetrating faculties of her genius, her childhood did not have the prominent details that make the pride of families. Only her beauty struck the gaze and necessitated attention; no speech revealed to people the range of her intelligence. If she perceived the admiration that her exterior attracted to her, she always seemed saddened and depressed by it.

Sometimes, in the evening, when she found her mother in sorrow, she approached without saying a word, sat down in the embrasure of a window, and, seeing the duke walking silently in the gardens, she took a harp and sang verses by Dante. At the first notes, magisterially enveloped by a profound richness of chords, Duchess Angelia became attentive and grave; the duke stopped. A magic was contained in the vibrations if that voice, in which the infernal and celestial thoughts were painted with the violence and relief of realities. However, the girl's face seemed impassive, and her eyes did not sparkle. Then, when they were still under the charm, she addressed a goodnight kiss to them, with a natural and humble submission.

Charity is one of the distractions of fortune; giving alms befits rich children. It flatters the self-esteem of parents and makes walks picturesque. For her, when the mysterious phenomena of alms arrived, she envisaged the poor at length. The instincts of depravity are often inscribed in faces racked by poverty; however, the child lowered her beautiful head and gave with humility. One might have thought that she was listening in the injured human form to receive herself the alms that she was giving and asking herself vaguely in the depths of her consciousness: "By what right is it given to me to make the head of that man or that woman curb? Why is it permissible for me to dispose of what it necessary to them?"

Her morning and evening prayer made her an angel—and yet, when she was alone in her oratory, when her mother was not praying beside her, she sometimes interrupted herself suddenly, raised her head and gazed fixedly at the venerable image of the Madonna, the giver of good death.

Once—she was then fifteen years old—in the middle of the prayer that she had prolonged every evening for a year, she stopped, seemed troubled, and advanced slowly toward a crucifix placed beside the Madonna. She remained before it in the silence of an indefinable meditation; then, two tears, the first ones she had shed in her life, ran down her face. A great pallor which she always conserved thereafter, was the sole indication of the vertigo she experienced; some time afterwards, she quit the oratory and no longer returned to it.

Her power of attention was concentrated on the evenings when the duke received old friends She noted in her memory the remarks of the old courtesans of the former reign, who had gone gray in European diplomacy and were far from having lost the thread of the various political cabinets in which their names had figured. Comments were made on many political events during those soirées in the form of witty conversation; she took an interest, in a certain measure, in those courses in the anatomy of history, and she learned the science of men and women at an age when young women are usually delivering themselves to occupations that are almost puerile.

That thirst to assimilate as much as possible, even things apparently foreign to her personal utility, went so far that one evening, having heard her father lauded as the foremost blade in Italy, she raised her eyes from the embroidery that he was holding for the sake of countenance, and appeared to consider him attentively. The next day, in a jesting and mocking manner, she asked him if he would consent to show her what he knew, in order to counter the fatigue of her tedious masters. It was a motive of filial respect that caused her to pretend to be bored by study, in order that her toil and continual late nights did not afflict her father and mother, or at least amaze them.

After a few words exchanged regarding the bellicose whim, the duke accepted. "She has it in her blood," murmured the old gentleman in his royalty—for a joke, because he was convinced that by the third lesson Tullia would lose interest. To his great astonishment, that was not the case at all, and he soon had occasion to marvel at his pupil.

They kept the secret of those combats; a torch fixed to the wall in one of the palace subterrains illuminated their passes of arms in the morning and the evening. It must have been a positively fantastic sight, that slender and wiry amazon clad in a black velvet smock, padded and armored like a fencer's plastron, tightened at the waist by a diamond cluster, breeches and sandals, her torrents of golden hair imprisoned by a net, and a steel trellis over her face, when she put herself graciously *en garde*, and saluted casually with a foil with a heavy ebony hilt.

After four years of exercises, close and savant assaults, her speed had achieved a lightning quality, and the pretty Queen Marguerite de Navarre might have appreciated the brilliant profundity of that Clorinda's swordplay.[1]

Those exercises had affirmed her supple form and preserved her health from being overwhelmed by work. Like the ancient virgins of Thebes and Sparta, she had modesty, beauty and strength. Science had lowered her forehead like an immortelle.

A charm of amiable grandeur ran through her merest speech. She only ever said simple things, and it was as if people became naïve before her sympathetic naïvety.

When she crossed the threshold of the immense apartment we are about to describe, however—where, for more than six years, she had shut herself away for eight or ten hours a day, not to mention the nights—the ingenuous amenity of her face fell away like a mask; the mysterious and somber splendor of her true personality appeared.

She went in, pushed the two bolts, came to set her elbows on a large black table laden with books, ancient manuscripts, maps and scientific instruments, and remained motionless.

There commenced the veritable life and the veritable aspect of Tullia Fabriana; the other was the one that everyone could see and forget.

---

1 Marguerite de Navarre (1492-1549) was the most influential woman in France after her brother became king Francois I in 1515. The female warrior Clorinda is a character in Tasso's *Gerusalemme Liberata* (1581), the French translation of which was widely used as a textbook in French schools in the nineteenth century.

Chapter VII

The Unknown Library

At every step of time, human intelligence
Opens, illuminating the darkness of phenomena,
Seizes more relationships
And taking from the fact the forces of life
Steals from matter, from its subjugating yoke
Laws and treasures.

Man explains the sphinx and the Theban stone;
He partly unveils the ebony breast of Africa
Under the gaze of its lions;
Blind Destiny sees by his experience;
He groups in the skies, around his science,
The constellations . . .
(Pontavice de Heussey, *Sillons et Debris.*)

THAT strange library was a treasure of rare and
curious books, extraordinary manuscripts and unknown documents. A good number of them bore rings
of religious armories; they came from cloisters in Italy,

Sardinia and Germany. Saved from the conflagration or pillage of convents, they had been collected, one by one, with study and patience, by two scholarly chaplains dead for a century.

Those two scholars had been attached to one of Duke Fabriano's ancestors; the latter had been occupied all his life with the occult sciences, philology, the Cabala and toxicology. He had spent fabulous sums thereon, and, in concert with the two chaplains, had made profound and magnificent discoveries. The unknown writings of those three men, disposed and accumulated with scrupulous method, filled a large ebony chest with a golden lock operated by secret springs.

Some of the books had been annotated in the margins by obscure Medieval monks, for the most part with reflections remarkable by virtue of their erudite precision. Between fifteen and twenty thousand volumes with antique bindings were accumulated on the shelves. Almost all of them revealed, on the part of the three thinkers, extensive knowledge of medicine and chemistry. All sorts of curiosities, fossils and equivocal objects brought back from voyages to distant countries, arranged here and there, testified to the care they had deployed in their scientific research. Almost undiscoverable editions were gathered there.

As antiquities, to begin with, there were authentic texts transcribed from the Samaritan Hebrew, the meaning of which, left without interpreters since the magi who alone possessed the veritable key, had been proposed in various fashions in remarks written by the monks.

There were also commentaries on the disappeared sciences of Egypt and the cult of idols, first imported by the black races, descendants of Ham, and reworked since by Aryans from Bactriana. There were also memoirs concerning the convulsionary populations of old North Africa, and the treatises of various Indianists on the revelations of beings that appeared in the subterranean ceremonies of ancient India, with citations in which were related, by the hands of ancient Brahmins, passages in Zend and Pahlavi taken from books that had disappeared completely.

Dusty folios circled with iron contained, according to their disquieting titles, the most profound and most ancient hypotheses on the subject of the recent appearance on the globe of humankind. Those archives were inestimable, and contained very particular secrets. It is notorious that we still do not know, today, the details concerning that question. The peoples from whom we might have been able to obtain information were already forgotten when scholars first began to occupy themselves with its clarification. The fall of primitive nations—or, if one prefers, their disappearance—followed their advent so closely that they did not have time to leave us anything positive in that regard, as one can be convinced by reading histories of the human mind in antiquity.

On the other hand, the Syriac legends imported by Druids coming from Asia, the poems of Scandinavian, Oceanian and Oriental literatures evidently do not lift in a sufficient manner the great shroud of sorts that covers things in their primordial state. We know by those accidents that almost all the libraries of the old world were lost.

There were also collections of Eutychian sentences, written in ancient Coptic, and inscriptions collected from ruins; remnants in black Ethiopian characters as ancient as the Deluge; and finally, the prophetic verses of the sibyls of Erythrae, Cumae and the Hellespont, inspired in Pindaric Greek, as harmonious as that of Homer, preceding the great volumes of magic.

The more recent books were separated from the others by instruments of chemistry, astrology and medicine. Numerous treatises could be remarked on almost all the sciences; the best volumes of history and metaphysics, as well as the summary of their progress as far as modern times; the sacred books of the eighteen great sects of the globe, with precious commentaries; the traditions of Slavic peoples on the origins of the great European nationalities; and, alongside the memoirs of the Academy of Physical Sciences of Florence, founded, as is well-known, by Cardinal de Medici—it appears that cardinals love to found academies—the works of the fathers of the Latin and Greek churches; and then, packed in age-old parchments, ligneous manuscripts in the Chaldean language, the annals of the stars, the history of the disappearance of some stars of old, of various celestial catastrophes as well as their signs and influence on human thought and universal destinies.

A modern man, at the sight of such vestiges, would simply say, almost involuntarily: "We've surpassed all that." The smile and the semi-respectful pleasantry with which he might have accompanied his reflection, the hint of polite and cool arrogance that would pierce his speech and manner, would betray the conviction of his superiority.

That is explicable. Ancient minds were, for the most part, systematically fixed minds; they had the fervor of their idea. Now, irresolution is the very essence of the air that our era respires. Men of immutable belief have the effect, with regard to the majority, of being ridiculous and antisocial. They are avoided with care.

The sentiment of the exact term is innate today, to the extent that the name of God, for example, seems to have been tacitly erased from conversation and philosophy. It is relegated to lexicons, sermons and books of piety. It has even become bad taste to risk pronouncing it, as the very Christian musketeers and gentlemen of the "great century" of France did. It is left tranquil, and almost no one makes use of it any longer, except in moments of danger, when it is thought appropriate to remember it; apart from that, the name of God is hardly ever employed except to close a dissertation in a dignified manner—which is to say, to dissimulate an indifferent caper.

Ah, it is the reign of doubt suckled with the milk of an artificial teat!

The astonishment of living leaps to the eyes so continually that the majority of men no longer worry about it and three-quarters of European thinkers no longer know what it signifies. It is incarnate, increasingly with every day that passes, with silent laughter, in the human drama. A particular species of indifference, of which the annals of history make no mention, is chilling the sentiment of duty in the hearts of individuals; the ineradicable disgust that floats overhead, retains the impetus of philosophers, scientists and artists in such a way that, apart from a few elite intelligences, a few last promoters if the human mind, scarcely anyone any longer has a heart for the work.

Lack of humility and hope has resulted in egotistical and devouring ennui. Progress has become dubious in its evidence and necessity; besides which, political economy, summoned to formulate a future possibility, if not satisfying, at least in rapport with our conscience, has only ended, after the most sublime efforts, in ridiculous darkness. No one is religious any more; everyone is timorous. There is no more youth and no more ideal. Anxiety has taken up residence in the family, in the law and in the future. Like the gods and kings, Art, Inspiration and Amour have fled! Countries attack one another and societies clash without understanding one another and without trying to understand. Rich and poor, workers and the workless, we are borne away into sorrow by a sepulchral wind of alarm and malaise.

The question of what Death reserves for us in its profundity has passed, for the majority of people, into an idle and insignificant state; the derisory sterility of analysis that every hypothesis on that subject presents, or appears to present, seems so intuitively obvious today that even mystics, in large number, allow themselves to be gained by the general lukewarmth.

In philosophy, however—although one curses privately the impotence in which one estimates it, perhaps gratuitously, to acquire in one fashion or another, after so many checks, any certainty regarding anything whatsoever—there is an incessant reflection on Death, everyone working in his own sphere of ideas and taking an interest in the phenomenon. One could say that Death has cast its shadow over the century. The hours of enthusiasm for the various branches of the tree of life, for distractions, secondary questions, arts, scientific discoveries, etc., have chimed. People are no longer moved.

The foresight of nature is great; she prepares her effects at length; one might say that humankind is suddenly going to sense a total, definitive surprise of some sort, and that, instinctively, it is reserving its strength in order to feel it.

However, the modern individual will probably think in advance, by what can we be seriously moved? Everything that the poetry and mythology of the ancients could imagine of the colossal and the strange has been surpassed by our reality. The gods no longer have our power; their thunder has become our plaything, our courier and our slave. The eagle's wings? The empire of the clouds? Do we not have hydrogen gas to mount excursions in the heavens? What Pegasus could follow an express train and contest breath with it? What Mercury could obey with the promptitude of an electric telegraph? What becomes of the Renown of a hundred trumpets before the millions of indefatigable voices of the press?

What figure would Neptune judge it appropriate to adopt in confrontation with our Leviathans, our harbor walls and our submarine chains? What would the rigid Rhadamanthus say at the sight of our great cities, so well policed? Phoebus-Apollo? But we have reduced him to "taking our picture," and made him our favorite painter. Hercules and his twelve labors make us smile;

for example, he killed the Nemean lion on his own; we have individuals who kill fifty lions for sport, single-handed. What astonishment would the physiognomy of Aesculapius show if he deigned to cast his eyes upon our treatises of anatomy, physiology, practical medicine and surgery?

The Muses? But do we not have women of letters, cantatrices, dancers and tragediennes, with regard to whom the comparison would not be to their advantage? Shall we talk about Eros, the Anacreontic Eros? The modern pathologist finds himself able to accord to dissolute old men monthly permission to deposit their "modest offering at the house of Venus." And as for Venus, we believe her to be, if not aged, at least over-rated. The man to whom it is given to see at more or less close range certain women of England, Circassia, Italy and Poland—not to mention France—scarcely admits the superiority of Venus.

As for the Empyrean, a leaf of Arabic hemp in a cigar, three pastilles of Egyptian hashish on the tongue or a few drops of brown opium in the carafe of a narghile, and we can see it as well, and perhaps better, than the gods. In any case, have we any need to create mirages of illusory worlds? Have we the desire? We go in search of them and discover them in reality, as witness the two Americas, Australia and the hundreds of islands of Oceania. Pindus and inaccessible Parnassus will support iron rails tomorrow, and the Hippocrene, the sacred fountain, will furnish excellent steam. The wisdom of Minerva will beat a retreat before German dialectics.

As for the god Mars, we would not want to humiliate his glorious club, but we believe that we can affirm one thing. Let us choose the *Iliad* as a subject, for example; the Greeks, furnished with ten or twelve kings, fifty or sixty thousand men and the help of the gods, required ten years to take Troy, and then it was to some hazardous, baroque and inadmissible ruse that they owed their success. Well, even if Achilles, Agamemnon, Ulysses, Ajax, son of Telamon or anyone else had joined Paris, Hector, Priam, etc. to defend it, and even if they had been commanded by all the gods, with Mars at the head, a detachment of artillery disembarked by steamboats from the Mediterranean, equipped with a dozen Congreve rockets, with a range of nearly two leagues, beating a breach at that distance, and as many mortars hurling bombs and rifled cannons, would have taken it in ten minutes.

Positively, the gods no longer have force with us on any species of terrain. The Titans are beginning to get the upper hand; the chains of old Prometheus, petrified on his Scythian rock, have rusted, and the eagle's beak is curved by old age. Is it not permissible, after all that, to infer that, little as human are, the gods are even less?

If Jupiter, for example, took it into his head to come back and play Amphitryon or to work miracles, he would simply be referred to one of the correctional police forces of Europe, and if he tried to escape, there would be instant extradition from all over the globe, which we handle like an apple nowadays. We are masters in our own home nowadays, and we have axes and thunder that the gods ought to fear, without giving the appearance.

That is certainly the reasoning that would have slumbered in the smile and the pleasantry of the modern individual we mentioned, and the arguments for the superiority that he would have been able to allege in order to legitimate his disdain or indifference with regard to the endeavors of the ancients.

The fact is that those arguments, in spite of the affected tone, appear to present, at first sight, a face so imposing and so somber that they take possession of the mind with the authority of evidence. They can go a long way! Whence comes, however, the impossibility that we experience in not hesitating before our glory, our labors and our divinity of recent date? We find it heavy, that divinity! To employ the expression consecrated by the vulgar, we must appear to be "*parvenus*" to the gods, so awkwardly do we behave.

In brief, perhaps it is a lack of habitude, but it will be hard for us to be gods.

We do not know what instinct comes to rally to the strongest our confidence in the future. The prodigies that surround us and the discoveries[1] of our perpetual

---

1 Author's note: "For example, it would be permissible to recall, among many others, the discovery of the vital force centralized in some knot of our marrow, some mode of activity of thought localized in some layer of cerebral pulp (in such a way that one can take away or put back at will the faculty of discerning, of willing, of suffering in the brain of an animal by removing or replacing a slice of its brain, as practiced today in Academies of Medicine); the more ancient discovery of independence and irritability; the discovery of the identity of solar metals with ours (a discovery obtained, as if well-known, by the chemical analysis of rays seized in a darkroom); the discovery of the sensibility of the magnet (by which the gesture of a living individual finds himself in immediate

labor, all give us a terrible and incontestable—by whom could it be contested?—sentiment of our value, awakening within us who knows what desperate conviction: an irremediable, infinite sorrow! The void envelops us obstinately; we cannot, in metaphysics, by only accepting reason, put our hand on the third term of the duality—if there is even a logical duality—any more than on living activity, in medicine. That escapes us, and the question seems liable to recoil indefinitely without ever being resolved, like mirages in deserts.

The new material metaphysics—we are talking about the most recent data from Germany—announces itself in such a way as to continue the state of doubt in which we are plunged: a profound sentiment, which appears indestructible, of the vanity of our condition of incessant struggle, within us, against the estimation of our task; it is no longer "what are we?" that it is necessary to say but "who are we?" Nevertheless, with regard to the question of being and nothingness, both having disappeared and formulated at the same time in some kind of eternal

---

contact, this time, with physics); the discovery of the reproduction of species by the creative forces of nature (which is to say, by the metallic and animate principles contained in a globule of blood, which, thrown into a vase filled with prepared liquid, causes hundreds of animals to develop there, becoming appropriate to our alimentation and provided with organs as perfectly formed as those obtained by ovarian generation); the discovery of Neptune in the heavens (a discovery confirmed forever by astronomy, as the discovery of America is confirmed by physical science); the discovery of the fusion of bones from one organism into another (thanks to which, in surgery, one can now substitute an animal bone for a human one in such a perfect manner that, after a time, the former absolutely replaces the latter); etc., etc."

becoming, the theory of Hegelian idealism seems devoid of appeal; the Antinomy that affirms the most abstract identity and opposition and demonstrates it as self-evident by reconstructing logically Nature, Humanity and Thought—forcing it, so to speak, to Appear and explain the reason for its explosion—by putting human Reason, in sum, on a par with the World-Spirit, has not been sufficiently shaken.

Alas, are we going to be the Becoming of God? How tedious!

Oh, why does the idea of our interior insufficiency dominate the presentiment of our immense destiny? Why can we not, when we dare to look ourselves in the face, simply resign ourselves to being *more than the gods*. If progress, the indefinite process, provides wellbeing, and, finding its justification in necessity, is the unique reason for existence, whence comes that lassitude—we do not say the negation—this almost universal malaise, this lack of enthusiasm for it? No one will propose that the movement in question corresponds to its abstraction and contains the first term of an ulterior determination; that necessity does not appear to us to be necessary. Whence comes the instinctive reaction of our consciousness, which determines that, while partly recognizing the evidence of Progress, everything within us sometimes allowing us admiration before the idea of its future profundity, we often deplore it and regard the spontaneous events of past consciousness, beliefs now reputed to be absurd, with sadness and sympathy?

Whence comes, we are saying, the mixed, extraordinary state that we have sensed weighing around us for a long time, the formula of which, in abstraction, would be capable of enabling us to doubt human Reason, logically sanctioning the *quia absurdum* of the mystics?

It is difficult to respond to that in a satisfactory manner; in any case, would it not be possible to add that an upheaval, an oscillation of the poles, a volcanic spasm, one of the earthquakes that are the periodic accidents of the globe, the condition *sine qua non* and the regime of the planet—revolutions that geology discovers by the thousand—that an accident of that nature, in sum, not to mention the hypothesis of an impact, henceforth very presentable, would be sufficient for all our progress to run a great risk of going to join, in its rank, the Assyrian civilizations, the empires of old worlds and the science of the hieroglyphite magi, in the supreme night of eternity?

Interlude[1]

IF one wanted to analyze attentively every scientific branch of progress, the idea of its importance and its general aspect might be greatly modified in minds, even the most determinedly partisan. Without establishing a theory of compensations—which, in any case, could never be rigorously exact because, in order to know an epoch, it would be necessary to be of that epoch—it would be easy, by holding to one's century, to find contradictions in the majority of the discoveries it presents. Let us take as a science the one that struggles against physical suffering and death, which often succeed one another: medicine.

It is certain that in modern times, physiological discoveries have assumed, unknown to the vulgar, expected

---

1 In the original printed text this essay is inserted, presumably as a belated improvisation, as an exceedingly long footnote, in parallel with the final paragraphs of the previous chapter. It seems to me to be legitimate and sensible to move it into a more comfortable location, with a more appropriate designation. Any reader who disagrees has only to reinsert the essay imaginatively in mid-sentence, immediately after the capitalized word Progress in the antepenultimate paragraph of the last chapter.

proportions capable, to the highest degree, of surprising the interest of thinkers. Never has precision in the art of curing been better obtained or more generalized, and no one is unaware that our pharmacies are richly endowed with everything that can lighten the burden of maladies.

In consequence, it is affirmed that the average duration of life has been augmented in several countries, and people go as far as furnishing figures of five, six or seven years.

However, the principle being posed that statisticians have only been to able offer exact figures for a century, on what solid, or even acceptable basis can any certainty be founded of that apparent extension of existence, especially when oscillations during that century are mentioned? How can those figures be reconciled with the totals obtained by statistics of poverty in Europe, totals whose annual progression rises in a sensible manner? How, finally, can that amelioration of the average duration of existence in our country be accorded with the immense quantities of alcohol, beverages and falsified aliments, with narrow and badly aerated dwellings, with the great neglect of hygiene, etc., etc.?

But we ought to set aside those objections, which do not bear upon the reality of the problem posed in all minds.

Philosophy, having no reasons of State, is only sincere in what it affirms, and scarcely admits those fashions of appreciating, or rather of gauging human life.

Duration is not life; it is one quality of it. Under the term "human life" we have the idea of action and thought. What enables a man to live is the bonds and relationships that unite him with his surroundings; the more those bonds fortify him, the more life is *realized* in the man. Now, what are the affections, the spontaneous and natural relationships that belong to him? Dreams or realities, we do not see more than four elements of life, elements in which pleasures, passions, duties go back six thousand years; they are the family, amour, conscience and the ideal. Since they are the natural elements of life, it remains to determine whether they are being reinforced in the civilized countries; in the affirmative case, we could propose that average life is in progress.

But we can see the reader's smile from here, so much is the result of the analysis known to him in advance. There is no need to write it. The types of the family are sufficiently mocked in Europe, every evening, in a thousand theatres, before a hundred million souls for one to be edified on the value attributed to that word by the majority. Amour has become something like the poetry of hygiene; the ideal can be defined, for the majority, as faith in the present. As for what concerns conscience and public morality, it is sufficient to open one of the Codes. Let us take that of France, for example. It includes about eighty thousand laws. We simply ask what conscience and public morality can there be in a country of thirty-eight to forty million souls, when it requires eighty thousand laws, a thousand tribunals always exuberant with affairs, five or six hundred thousand bayonets and forty or fifty thousand policemen to maintain them?

The average duration of life is augmenting? In supposing that, it is necessary to confess that the augmentation in question costs dear. Humans have wanted to liberate themselves from old prejudices; they desire to "purify their ideal," in sum, to become *free*, according to their indefinable expression. In that they are served as they wish; there is no longer anything but the artificial. Crimes are also diminishing—but vices are augmenting, and humans always arrive at losing in depth what they gain in surface area.

Let us return to medicine. In confrontation with a decisive question—that of human blood, for example—science appears to be troubled. In defining the various modes of manifestation, the numerous symptoms under which its weakening appears, by the vague and general term chlorosis,[1] one finds, according to the estimates of enlightened practitioners and according to the census of modern maladies, that millions of chloroses can be counted in Europe; which induces one to think that, whatever the enthusiasts of erroneous and embryonic statistics might say, the forces of constitution are decreasing in human generations by reason of the intellectual development of societies.

It might be objected that "the remedy follows the disease." One might mention, for example, the discovery of the treatment of chloroses with iron. Disinterested individuals answer for the efficacy of iron. On two subjects chosen and treated in identical conditions with iron—

---

1 Most of what was generally known as "chlorosis" in 1863 would nowadays be called anemia, but the latter term is more specific in its range and implication.

presented in any formula, as a lactate, iodide, citrate, etc., it does not matter—the result might be the death of one and the cure of the other without it being possible to determine the reason for the difference. What escapes medical experimentation has the same nature as what escapes metaphysics, and what are called elements, forces and principles do not respond to that title; they are inexact words, nothing more.

Elements? How is it, then, that having all the elements of human blood, not a drop can be distilled? How is it that it is permissible to mix nitric acid, graphite, water etc., indefinitely without obtaining flesh with that composition? How is it that one can manipulate phosphates of magnesium, chalk and soda, combining them with the rest of the elements left by the decomposition on all the parts of a skeleton without succeeding in fabricating bone by that means? What are the impotent principles that need something other than themselves, it appears, to produce their consequences?

All that reminds us of a well-known saying of one of the most illustrious and most profound doctors of recent times; on his death-bed he formulated his trivial and supreme conclusion thus: "Keep the head cool, the feet warm and the belly free, and make a mockery of physicians." The joke of a moribund, agreed, but are there many physicians who could say as much? It is noticeable in addition that those who doubt a science are almost always those who appear to have made that science the goal of their career.

In sum, the newest and clearest thing that medicine has discovered is that a sober and regular diet, healthy aliments, exercise, pure air, calm morals and a good temperament can enable one to live to a hundred. Unfortunately, that excellent maxim, which our first parents thought they ought to bequeath to us, while remaining the fundamental axiom and definitive conclusion of science, has become very difficult to put into practice for five people out of six. Increasing populations, economic difficulties, the strange organization of trades, means of existence and the modern way of life exclude and put out of reach for millions of souls even the possibility of practicing a suitable hygiene. Condemned to suffer the worst maladies more frequently than the ancients, we shall gradually arrive at a universal system of cures and drugs that will render generations debilitated, impoverish human vitality and, finally, hasten the appearance of a second terminus in the progression of duration. Who can say, in fact, the statistic of life is not suspended on two termini, on an ascending and descending progression, like everything else, and that we are marching toward the first terminus of a period of diminution?

It is evidently certain—for those who, reducing at a glance all the petty arbitrary aberrations to their common denominator, knowing that an indefinite radiation of stupidities can stem from as word deviated from its real acceptance—that, taking account of the natural increase of populations, mortality follows with its ordinary and punctual fidelity the progression of numbers, as of old. The number and variety of maladies is augmented in hidden germs as humans create habitudes, consequences of other branches of progress, and the explosion of an imminent collapse certainly ought not to be considered as absolutely impossible.

Not only did the ancients surpass us, as moderns admit, in their hygienic theories but in the art of curing their sick, experience appearing to demonstrate that they succeeded in the same proportion as us. It is necessary, moreover, not to omit that even in our day, anchorites lost in deserts, the empirics and conjurers of the Orient and the dervishes of Egypt, etc., also have their extra-scientific methods of curing the most horrible diseases that have ever afflicted our species, and in a much more rapid and radical fashion than the physicians of Europe can cure them.

It goes without saying that we cannot enter here into the smallest developments, and that it is not even permitted to us to indicate in a summary fashion the state of a single actual question. We regret being obliged to pass on quickly, and have no other pretention, in these notes, than that of formulating in broad strokes a possible point of view.

Medicine is linked to chemistry in such a way that one can suggest that the former is a facet of the latter. Let us take a detail of that new science. We have arrived in chemistry at summarizing the mystery—or at least one of its abstract parts—of hydrogen; it is almost certain today that the atomic weight of all substances is an exact multiple of its own. Now, what is hydrogen? A quality! Always qualities, never principles. "That is the motto and justification of indefinite progress," cry the hundred or two hundred million men who populate from morning till evening the three hundred thousand cafés of Europe, and who have the goodness, after having ruminated synthetically an indigestible mass of periodicals, humbly to set the tone for the human mind. It is sufficient to affirm what they say to see its uncertainty. In all that, certainly, there is something very beautiful and very mysterious; it is the seriousness of humanity creating a logic in everything, without knowing why or how, but as astronomers prey to the grip of we know not what celestial alarm said recently: "Is it good to have reason and not to have the time to reason?"

Oh, we amuse ourselves in the darkness pushing it back by insignificant decimals; we believe that we understand a phenomenon because we name it in accordance with some condition of our language, as if that were its true name. Things remain as hidden as before and we really cannot see clearly anywhere in this century of enlightenment, as witness the two scientists who, stupefied by a question of physics, said to one another—some people heard the fact cited in 1861 by an eminent rationalist during a course in chemistry at the College de France, in front of the planet and scientific humankind—"Even the absurd might not be impossible."[1]

That, then, is the supreme cry to which reason is constrained to utter continually today, after six thousand years of labors and dreams, which cannot help engendering certain reflections on the subject of the authenticity of progress.

---

1 The previously-cited Ernest Renan gave his inaugural lecture at the Collège de France in December 1861, but this quotation from a course in chemistry is far more likely to have originated from Marcellin Berthelot.

Let us add, in passing, that we have very few spectacles capable of competing in splendor with Babylon, Memphis, Tyre, Jerusalem, Nineveh, Sardis, Thebes, Ecbatana, etc., etc., and that, with regard to esthetics, the moderns yield to the ancients. On the other hand, the club of old Cain is disguised, but the arrow, the sword and the cannon are equivalent in value; as engines of murder are universalized, superiority disappears; progress becomes compensation. "We are marching toward the abolition of wars," say the "broadeners of the intellectual horizon." It is necessary to admit that we have not seen much thus far.

Humans are not nourished by bread alone; what has become of the ideal? We no longer find it anywhere, even in the heavens. Like Olympian Jupiter, the thinkers do not deign to see anything. Well, far from us is the absurd idea of denying progress heavily; a man who puts one foot in front of the other is making progress. But that the progress can emerge from a very restricted circle, or demonstrate anything other than our indefinite dependence and final ignorance, it is permissible to doubt. The science of the ancients is reckoned too cheaply; we willingly imagine a great difference between their philosophical level and ours. It remains to be determined whether the calm on the subject of the idea of God is a progress, which no one can demonstrate in a very clear manner. The immensity is as unknown to them as it is to the rest of us, and in recalling the slightest detail of astronomy, one perceives that they occupy themselves methodically and fervently to the great question.

For example, two thousand years ago, to cite one fact among a thousand, an observer of Alexandria,[1] having invented the modern armillary sphere and fixed, very nearly, the obliquity of the ecliptic, obtained for the arc of the meridian comprised between the tropics an expression with which present-day science can only find an insignificant inexactitude. In truth, the steps that we have made in almost all the sciences can be represented by the difference between two decimal points in a calculation of twenty centuries ago and ours. Four thousand two hundred years ago the Chaldeans found their lunar triple saros by means of necessarily complicated calculations.

The Jews were well aware of the period of our years, which is claimed by us to have been discovered by some Scythian or Lapp monk in the year 500 of our era; it is sufficient to cast an eye over their books to see it. Three thousand years ago the Chinese noticed the mobility of the ecliptic by observing the needle of a sundial, and the invention of the sundial is lost in the night of history. Two thousand two hundred years ago, the Babylonians discovered further ingenious varieties. The discovery of the precession of the equinoxes dates from two thousand three hundred years ago; without the pretended "hazard" that enabled us to "discover" optics five hundred years ago—which goes back three thousand years, according to the optical treatises of Ptolemy—and, in consequence, the refractions of light, we would not know much more than the ancients about astronomy.

---

1 Eratosthenes.

And what do we know, in spite of that? We know a few million stars as well as a part of the phenomena of their various evolutions. The children of today, more analytical than little Chaldean shepherds, can, by dividing a second of a degree in the displacement of a ray of light, know the distance that separates us from each of them and weigh the substance that composes them by calculating the force of their mutual attraction. The affirmation that the entire solar system—the Universe, as one says—only weighs a sextillion pounds, if it is true that two and two make four could even, according to us, awaken a smile whose agreed skepticism would not be exempt from horror.

Yes, we have analyzed the sheaf of luminous angles that a ray traveling nearly a hundred thousand leagues a second comes to project on our eye after having traveled, for at least ten years, the vast abysms of the ether and ten thousand kilograms of the atmosphere, the pressure of which the human eye supports, and we have improved our lenses, invented polariscopes, gradually brought the heavens closer; which comes down to saying, fundamentally, that we enjoy, thanks to our powerful instruments, obtained by so much labor, blood and late nights, a slightly better view than that of the Germans who, science says, distinguished by eye one of the satellites of Jupiter and the rings of Saturn, and who marked with pencils in hand the distances of nebulae. Perhaps the telescope is like the crutch of our weakened and sick eyes. Who knows how far the first humans could see naturally? Whether the world is six thousand years old or as many billions of centuries, all that is of equal value under reflection that it is still necessary to come to the commencement—which is to say, the non-sense, the mystery, the memorial, the absurd. The data that we have today in the detail of the sky, or its general laws, might perhaps be overturned tomorrow by other data and other laws—and that is all of our substratum.

Already, criticisms are rising in a sufficiently specious manner to be worthy of attention.

Although the majority of astronomers regard the firmament as the anatomist regards a cadaver, it nevertheless remains superbly unknown. One can say, however, that the public no longer has time to think about it. We scarcely sense its divine vertigo occasionally! The Chaldeans conceived the grandeur of relationships that we can unite in silence! "The imaginations of vulgar pastors," it is said. But all reality supposes an anterior imagination that thought it. Where does imagination begin and end? What one sees either is or is not; if it is not, how is it that it can be seen? If, on the contrary, it is, what more can the reality of a body add to it for us, since everything ends up disappearing for us?

Oh, the children of Chaldea, wandering over the mountains in the nocturnal wind, sensed clearly the poetry that is the consciousness of nature, and they were right to attach, with a gaze of faith surprising future progress, their obscure destinies to the luminous curse of a star, thus creating, throughout the infinity of their thought, an irrevocable relationship between their humility and its sublimity.

Chapter VIII

Isis

Seek and ye shall find . . .
Verily, I say unto you: the man who wants
to conserve his life will lose it; the man
who wants to give it will find it again.
(Jesus Christ.)[1]

A T twenty years and a half, Tullia Fabriana found
herself alone in the world.

The tendency of her mind to profound meditations—a tendency that, physiologists say, almost always
accompanies in a woman a complexion disposed to
sterility, was already so aggravated in her that her senses,
still new, did not solicit her.

The most attractive distractions appeared to her
to be of scant value, her labors having been sufficient

---

1 A compound of *Matthew* 7:7 and 16:25, the latter repeated in
Luke 17:33, but slightly altered in Villiers' version, which I have
back-translated.

to satiate her in advance of pleasures, triumphs and amours. The most somber disdain began to fill her heart; in spite of her indifference, she thought that, being beautiful, it might happen that she was loved, and as she no more intended to feel the joys of divided love than the sorrows of solitary love, she found herself to be a human exception.

Then she decided on a distance; she isolated herself, without withdrawing entirely, without ceasing to do as much good as possible around her with the larger part of her immense fortune, and only accepting from outside the respect of her name.

In the meditation of her retreat, she dreamed magnificently about herself and about the world, and abandoned herself entirely to the sublime attractions of Thought.

To cast a rapid disillusioned glance into the depths of her alarming science, to summarize it from the viewpoint of nature and history, to succeed in linking, by means of a series of connections, the perspectives and fine detail of all those observations, including the philosophical question, was the work of a few months for her redoubtable intelligence.

One evening, determined to think by herself, she closed her heavy volumes of metaphysics and leaned her elbows, as always, on her study table.

"Sphinx! You, the most ancient of the gods," murmured the beautiful Promethean virgin, "I know that your realm is similar to the arid steppes, and that it is necessary to march for a long time in the desert to reach you. Ardent abstraction does not frighten me;

I shall try. In the temples of Egypt, the priests placed next to your image the veiled statue of Isis, the figure of Creation; on the pedestal they had inscribed the words: *I am all that is, was, and will be; no one has lifted the veil that covers me.*[1] Under the transparency of the veil, the dazzling colors of which were sufficient for the eyes of the crowd, only the initiates were able to sense the form of the stone enigma and, at intervals, they added further layers of multicolored pleats, in order to make it increasingly impossible for human eyes to profane her. But centuries have passed over the veil, fallen into dust; I shall cross the sacred enclosure and I shall try to look at the problem intently."

At the moment of entering into the realm of solitary meditation, the young woman was surprised to turn her head and cast a mild gaze, for the first time, over the dream of life. Yes, for the first time, she would have liked to believe, to love, to forget! But soon, disdainful and grave, she resisted firmly and extended all the power of her mind toward the most vertiginous summits of the ideal.

Days and nights passed.

According to the symbolic poem,[2] Satan, having forced the doors of Hell, looked into the darkness and launched himself into its depths in search of Eden. His wings beat in the void that his gaze explored. Thus, the

---

1 I have back-translated Tullia's version of the inscription alleged by Plutarch to have appeared on a statue of Isis or Neith in Sais, which differs slightly from other translations of the original text.
2 Milton's *Paradise Lost*.

soul, having escaped its cell,[1] by means of the consciousness of identity,[2] precipitates itself into the mystery of Being[3] in order to find there the cause and the reason of ulterior determinations, realizes that conception.

How many systems, annihilated as soon as they appeared, blazed before that spirit!

Days and nights passed.

Something quite remarkable! Considerations resulting from a point of view sufficiently distant from the one where the majority of women habitually place themselves, induced her not to forget the exteriority of her person, in spite of her terrible studies—in sum, not to neglect herself physically. She decided in favor of a way of life sustained by a method whose secrets she had

---

1 Author's note: "The Self. See Fichte, *Logic*. See also *Treatise on Sensations* by Abbé de Condillac and Lélut, *The Physiology of Thought*." The first reference is to a translation of excerpts from Fichte published in France in 1812 as *Logique transcendantale*. Étienne de Condillac's *Traité des sensations* was published in 1754 and François Lélut's *Physiologie de la pensée* in 1862.

2 Author's note: "See Schelling, *Transcendental Idealism*, but do not take account of his notes, in *An Appreciation of the Works of Cousin*, on the subject of Hegel, in which the following proposition is found: 'That which is is the primitive; its being is only ulterior, etc.' since this is no necessity, does not prove anything, and does not think any more than Hegel's proposition." Friedrich Schelling's *System des transcendentalen Idealismus* was first published in 1800 and translated into French in 1842.

3 Author's note: "See Hegel, *Logic*, *The Science of Being*. The identity of being and nothingness, considered in themselves, empty and undetermined. People who do not now German can consult Monsieur Véra's beautiful translation, one of the philosophical monuments of the century." Augusto Véra's *Introduction à la philosophie de Hégel* was published in 1855, followed in 1859 by the two volume *Logique de Hégel*, the collection cited.

studied and which conserved her magnificent pallor of white roses and the freshness of her beautiful blood. It is well-known that Italian climes, and, in general, almost all those of southern countries, favor and even impose hygienic abstinence; hence the sobriety with which the common people live in Italy, and their constant privation of fortifying aliments does not harm their nature; thanks to the nourishing atmosphere that they respire, they are as healthy as those of the North.

As Fabriana intended to maintain her mind in the marvelous state of lucid health in which it was, not only would the idea of gastronomic pleasures have carried her away, but, seconded by the climate of Florence, she was obliged to adopt a diet of a severity that only her marble constitution could find very good.

She never drank anything but cold water gilded with a few drops of elixir; by night, when she was very hungry, she made do with a little bread, sometimes ice cream, oranges and tea; she rarely desired anything more succulent.

That asceticism spared her the wasted time and ennuis of malady, and she always found herself reposed.

She got up, bathed in the gardens enveloped in a peplum, a garment in which she found herself more at ease and more rapidly dressed; then she came into the library, lay down on a sofa, thought for long hours without quitting her attitude, leaning her elbow on the cushions, except for leafing through a book of philosophy or mathematics occasionally and scanning a passage. She never pronounced a word; her half-closed eyes did not shine; no sign of admiration, dread or hope ever made her shudder; only drops of sweat pearled on her temples, sometimes rolling as far as her eyelashes, like sublime tears; and then, like the great Isis, she wiped them away with her veil.

Days and nights passed.

Meanwhile, the sun was radiant over the countryside; children loved one another in the forests. Nature was peaceful; the spring of her youth recited to her, in the voice of its heavenly breezes, in the perfume of its flowers swollen with sap, the melancholy song of the ancients: "Cynthia, the days and nights are flowing away; you are forgetting to live; do you not want to do as the children are doing, since you are young and beautiful?"[1]

Her late nights were sometimes prolonged until the morning, always in that profound mutism, in the intensity of abstraction that no exterior sign betrayed, and which, in two years of identity, had become something frightening; her slumber had evidently to be a continuation of fatigue. How far had that woman plunged? Was it possible to admit, with regard to such energy, that she was dreaming at random, allowing herself to be dazzled by all the mirages of objectivity? No, no! The great solitary, of brief and robust thought, had to know what she was doing. The Immemorial mystery that forms, according to us, the foundation of the world, could not have escaped her consciousness or her intelligence; perhaps, having reached her height, she was seeking a point of departure more satisfying than Necessity.[2]

---

1 The fickle and demanding Cynthia was the Muse and principal subject-matter of the Latin poet Propertius.

2 Author's note: "This is said under the Hegelian criterion, and

One incident that might have been very grave and very unfortunate for her existence, and which we ought to report because of the purely poetic character with which it was enveloped, arrived in her existence toward the end of the third year.

One night, Tullia Fabriana, enclosed and isolated in her thought, as always, was sitting at her table; an iron lamp, placed next to her, left the depths of the apartment in obscurity, but illuminated fully the tranquil physiognomy whose entirely interior gaze appeared to be contemplating unknown firmaments.

Oh, the invisible world! The *thing* that troubles in spite of its insignificant contingency! It was a filthy night, heavy and swollen with storms. Like distant howls uttered in that direction by the planet, the convulsions of electricity were prolonged in the mountains. The sky had tints of gold, jet and bistre; immense clouds were arriving in great haste; the young woman could hear those dull impacts, distant and confused, whose murmur, carried by the rain and lukewarm wind that entered through the open casements. One might have thought that exterior nature wanted to warn the attentive ear fixed upon it somewhere.

Suddenly, she got up. It was the first gesture of her meditation! Her profound dark eyes shone like two flames. Her face was as pale as death.

In the great library there was a celestial sphere of colossal dimensions; she found herself placed in front of a vast glazed window, wide open. The night, set ablaze by

---

with a reservation whose explanation will be given in the second volume of his work."

lightning, with a marvelous life, caused to sparkle like veritable stars the innumerable golden and silver stars incrusted on the enormous blue ball. A spiral with velvet steps surrounded that sphere; at the summit, on a narrow platform, two or three cushions were thrown, and astronomical instruments were scattered on the cushions.

The lamp was burning on the table.

Tulia Fabriana—doubtless the storm had indisposed her momentarily—put her hand to her forehead. To see the fixed impression of her gaze, it became presumable that the sky, the earth and the night were far from her thought, and that she did not know or understand anything of what was happening around her.

She approached the sphere with a slow step, climbed the steps, and, throwing the compasses on the carpet, she tottered. Her tunic, unfastened like a mantle, slid along her body; her undone hair enveloped her, and in the glimmers of the night, it resembled a radiance.

She appeared, white and luminous, without remarking the depth of the storm and the darkness, and without paying any head to the brutal black space. She appeared, like the goddess of those nights of horror in which those who seek do not find.

But what was she thinking? To what astonishments could her mind have abandoned itself for the first time.

At that very moment, with a hideous flash, a thunderbolt came into the apartment through the open window.

The fluid threw her down, unconscious, on the porphyry sphere. She remained flat on her back, her limbs extended, her hair floating, her eyes closed, in the midst of the monstrous commotion of the thunder.

By means of one of those efforts, one of those absurd and fortunate prodigies that lightning sometimes commits, she was not wounded. No harm was done, but the shock having been of great violence, she remained motionless for several hours, as if overwhelmed. Apart from that fatigue, the electricity left her no memory of its visit.

When she came round, it was broad daylight; the weather was superb; the good odor of the grass after the storm embalmed the air. She raised herself up on her elbow, dreamed for a few moments, then got up and descended on to the carpet.

Once dressed, she went to the window, looked at the trees, the sky, the flowers and the immense space.

"Five hours lost!" she said, very softly.

That was all, and a few minutes later, she appeared to have forgotten the terrible incident that had just troubled her because of the imprudence that she had committed in leaving the windows open on stormy nights.

A few days later she changed her way of life completely. She spent days alone, on horseback, riding through the vales, and only returning to her palace in the evening.

Since that extraordinary night, her features had taken on the expression of a statuesque tranquility; one might have thought that it was not fatigue that had made her get up with a start, and that it was not the storm that had paled her! She appeared simply to be following, since her awakening, the immense enchainments of a unique thought.

One day, she returned to the library. She opened one of the volumes of magic, and after long hours, having aligned several figures in the margin with her pencil, she said "Very well!" in a low voice, and added dully: "I'll wait."

Days and nights passed.

She did not lose sight of the world; the world could not trouble her. She attended soirées and balls quite willingly. She held her superb rank there.

She chatted, without ennui, about the usual things and details and smiled graciously in the midst of jovial repartee. Those brilliant friends and dancers certainly did not suspect that their compliments and speech were falling into her profound soul as the sounds of the bells of hamlets fall in winter, carried away by distant nocturnal squalls into the desolation of space . . .

Given that sudden whim for distractions it might have been possible to think that, weakening like others before the Problem, she had secretly renounced crossing the passage; but she had a double aspect; her fixed gaze, her immobility in solitude, and that simplicity in society, that insouciant elegance of speech, testified by their combination that she had a reason for acting in that way and that her idea had passed into the sphere of action.

A genius does not accept discouragement; that is why he is a genius. He is like a soldier struck in the excitement of the melee, who, not perceiving his blood loss, continues marching upon the enemy and only stops at the moment when he notices death, which is to say, when his duty is terminated.

Tullia Fabriana's thought could not have flinched in the abyss; it was obvious that, like the diver in the ballad, she was bringing the golden cup back to some unknown king.[1]

Now, it was past! The struggle was over; the angel was vanquished. The mortuary shrouds of anguish, the vast fear of despair and the sublime ecstasy of eternal life, all formed in the depths of her soul a somber mass of memories. She was like a voyager returning from unknown lands. Her grave forehead had the beauty of the night; she was the queen of vertigo and darkness. The earth, its climes and races, must have appeared to her like rapid and fantastic visions on a canvas. Perhaps she had discovered, at the summit of some stupefying law, the living panorama of forms of Becoming; perhaps the abstraction, by virtue of splendors, had taken on for her the proportions of the supreme poetry.

In all certitude, such a soul could not be duped by its shadow, and if she had posed somewhere, if she had held on to something, it was because it was what she needed. It could not have been for the sole pleasure of following ideas in flight that she had determined to skirt madness, *delirium tremens*, the fevers of hallucination and the entire cortege of Thought for every hour of the day and night for three years.

She had reached the height where sensations are prolonged internally to the vanishing point; there were familiar rapprochements of her present actions with

---

1 The reference is to a ballad by Schiller, "Der Taucher (1797; tr. as "The Diver"), set to music by Franz Schubert.

confused memories. Warnings came to her from everywhere, silently, from the Impersonal. Those phenomena posed before her thought as if before an impassive mirror; an unexpected obscurity weighed upon her slightest actions; it seemed to her that she distinguished, without effort, the point at which the profundities of banal life were connected to the dreams of an invisible world, so that the details of every day, having become definite, had a distant significance for her soul . . .

She was twenty-four years old. She had traveled, compared, meditated on social laws, learned the details of great causes; from the day when she had spoken alone, her will appeared to have taken possession of an obsession. She resumed seeing society, seeing it in a sequential and calculated manner.

Three years went by, and after those three years, at twenty-seven, anyone who had penetrated her intimate life would have been surprised to recognize a new and very singular aspect to it.

Once, in that time, a circumstance whose obscure origin seemed to be attached to questions of scant importance to her had implicated her in a vast and royal intrigue in which she had accepted the most difficult role and which she had brought to fruition.

She had taken advantage of it, by means of presence of mind, to appropriate inestimable secrets. In addition to her fortune, the origin of which was sufficiently recognized and definite, she had in her memory another fortune and a great power. On sounding further, one would have discovered something marvelous, which is that, by means of practical skill, elevated relations and knowledge of detail, she had ended up very rapidly, without being remarked, dominating, without any noise and as if in play, almost all the men of value disposing of material force in Italy.

That hidden power extended as far as the Roman States. From the depths of her palace, she exercised over the various acts of government the supremacy that she had acquired, with a view to an indefinable goal. She had doubtless determined the results to come, but their depth escaped her most subtle creatures. Those who served her by virtue of tacit obligations or interested hopes, were far from suspecting their number. More than that, in politics she passed, in the eyes of the most clairvoyant, for an indifferent woman or of ordinary range; for, by means of a magisterial strategy of dissimulation, she succeeded in allowing it to be believed that everyone was acting for himself. She wrote little, and that is why her letters were more compromising for those who received them than for her.

First she repeated word for word the request that was made of her, which specified clearly and without any possible ambiguity the exact meaning of the response. Now, firstly, if the question had not been posed in sufficiently precise terms to be able, if necessary, to become a weapon in expert hands, she responded in a vague and brief fashion; secondly, if she judged that someone was sufficiently delivered to her, she sent back a pure and simple yes or no, on the reverse side, in such a way that the response could be shown without the request. Thus, she always remained free and sure of herself. That method had the great strength that it disconcerted the suspicions of those who might believe a certain scope of designs, since she rendered them their weapons; but no one thought of that consequence.

She avoided by that means the various commentaries to which the conduct of a woman whose influence is feared is exposed because, only being in her hire, no one was in haste to make a show of it, supposing inferiority.

There was little noise in diplomacy, therefore around her name. The solid mesh of the net with which she enveloped, in obscurity, a good part of the decrees of imperial or Roman politics, ended on her finger at a supreme ring, which she moved from time to time.

Although, during her travels, she only appeared at long intervals at the great receptions of nuncios, official soirées at the consulates or prefectures of Austria and flamboyant balls at the embassies of France, England and Spain; although the welcome with which she was accepted there would never have given rise to suspicion of links of more deference than that due to her rank, she could have predicted almost infallibly the day when some decree would be signed by a pontiff, a parliament, a queen or an emperor.

What was she proposing to attain? What did she want to bring about? Of what importance were those maneuvers to her, whose habits and strange tastes put her existence beyond any social conflict; to her, who had no desire to augment her position or be useful to anyone, with no patriotic illusions? What was the point of the permanent, subterranean web that she wove coldly for three or four years? It was impenetrable.

At any rate, her plan, whatever it was, remained enveloped in darkness and inattention because of that fashion of acting.

It was, therefore, to the home of that extraordinary woman that Prince Forsiani and his young friend Count Wilhelm had come that evening. They were waiting in a drawing room.

Chapter IX

The Introduction

Almanazor, ferry here the commodities
of the conversation.
(Molière, *Les Precieuses.*)[1]

THE marchesa entered.

The drawing-room overlooked the gardens. Before the large open casements, the curtains were moving slightly. White flagstones took the place of a carpet or parquet. Silvery gauze dust-covers knotted at the end of torsades enveloped the ceiling chandeliers. Here and there were heavy chairs in sculpted ebony, upholstered in black velvet, and a similar sofa, near a window. On the somber paneling, magnificent paintings by Guido Reni and Titian stood out in their golden frames. A torchère full of candles placed behind a marble basin from which large sprays of natural flowers escaped, il-

---

1 The full title of Molière's one-act farce is *Les Précieuses ridicules* [The Ridiculous Affected Women] (1659). Almanazor is a lackey of the two young women to whom the title refers.

luminated the apartment. The high mantelpiece with extinct candelabra supported a large clock in Florentine bronze; armoried panels indicated doors to the other drawing rooms of the palace.

The two gentlemen were standing opposite a painting.

Tullia Fabriana saluted them with a movement of the head, half-smiling. The prince bowed, with an amiable negligence, a perfectly measured tact and taste. Wilhelm also bowed, but troubled, as if by a dazzle.

The marchesa came toward the window, with a sign of approach. Prince Forsiani took the young man by the hand.

"Madame Marchesa," he said, "I have the honor of presenting to you the Count of Strally-d'Anthas."

Both men sat down before the young woman. She was leaning back, her hands half-joined, her elbow resting on one of the arms of the sofa.

"Didn't you say yesterday evening, Milord, that you were to quit us tonight?" she asked.

"Yes, Madame; and if a few cares cause you anxiety at the court of Naples, will I be fortunate enough to be watchful there in your place?"

"The Queen has done me the honor of writing to me last week, and two lines added by Lord Acton expressed some urgency on the subject of an immediate response. Several difficulties have not permitted me to satisfy him before this evening. I simply desire to offer Her Majesty my regrets for not being able to be useful to her in the circumstances of which she speaks, and since you leave me to dispose of your complaisance . . ."

Prince Forsiani bowed. "My absence will not be long, I hope," he added

While Fabriana was speaking, Wilhelm had fallen prey to a phenomenon of cold horror. That *voice*, the velvet contralto timbre, was not unknown to him, that was certain.

But it seemed to him—and the intensity of the sentiment had taken on the proportions of an evident reality within him—that it had been long ago, in the impalpable past, in a land struck by a silence without echoes, a terrible silence, in forgotten ages of which he could not conceive the date, that it had been in that void that he had heard the *voice*. He recalled the singular confidences of the prince in the Casines, and had sufficient empire over himself to keep a straight face.

That hallucination only lasted a moment. *I was dreaming*, he thought, and did not worry about it any more.

They talked about random matters for a few minutes, and then returned to current affairs. At an allusion that Prince Forsiani appeared to advance on the subject of peace or war, the marchesa looked at him.

"Your Excellency will pardon me," she said. "I don't desire to know any details, but I thought that the embassy had motives of a different order in view."

"Those motives touch the gravest interests," Forsiani replied. "The question of the finances of Naples is very obscure; the bonds, doubtless because of the excessive expenditure of the court, have fallen into such a sorry discredit today that a rich Jew, for example, if he were able to purchase in a certain fashion, could install himself, perhaps tomorrow, on the throne of Gonzalvo di Cordova.[1] That would realize a rather sad miniature of those bankers of ancient Rome who trafficked imperial power. That, however, is the result toward which we are heading."

"Oh?" said Tullia Fabriana, still impassive.

"I believe so," added the prince. "In truth, these questions end up dominating all others; peoples threaten, the future darkens."

"That's true," said the marchesa, "and I've had an amusing idea. If, by some miracle, all flags flying, a fleet arrived from Heaven—a little like the supreme manna that the Hebrews once took such great care to collect—do you think that King Ferdinand would refuse it?"

It was the prince's turn to look at Tullia Fabriana. "Resignation to the thrusts of Heaven is a royal virtue, beautiful lady," he replied.

"Resignation! According to your words, would it be very surprising if His Sicilian Majesty were required to practice it seriously, perhaps soon? Is it forbidden to suppose the existence of those who are able to buy things with steel, iron and lead, for want of more precious metal?"

She started to laugh.

---

1 "Gonzalvo di Cordova" was the nickname of Gonzalo Hernadez y Aguilar, who assisted the King of Naples, Ferdinand II, to drive out the French in 1498 and became known as "El Gran Capitan." He subsequently won that kingdom for Spain—an achievement for which he obtained scant gratitude from the jealous king of Spain, but endured until 1788, when the present story is set; the Bourbon Ferdinand IV ruled Naples then, in a time of turbulent diplomacy, as indicated by Tullia's commentary.

"Lamberto Viscontis are rare, Madame; such examples have become so difficult to follow. To wager one's life on a throw of the dice against the advantage of being king is no longer such an attractive proposition."

"Do you think so, Signor Strally?" asked the marchesa, smiling.

"Madame," Wilhelm replied, "I esteem that merely finding oneself in a position to make the wager is a precious favor of destiny."

"And would you be saddened by your fate if, having tried, you lost?"

"No, Madame."

"What did I tell you, Prince?"

Wilhelm's soft voice, and the natural quality of his accomplished bearing, excluded any idea of ostentation from his responses. He was a great lord, he spoke simply. The trouble and the ardent emotion that he was suppressing were only transparent for Fabriana alone, in an intuitive and veiled manner. The diplomat, knowing the world, wondered: *Can he be absolutely indifferent?* But he did not pause on that idea.

At that moment, a charming young woman dressed in a Greek costume came in, placed on a table a silver-plated tray laden with iced liqueurs and retired silently.

"Will you accept?" Fabrina said, graciously.

They refused with a hand gesture.

"So," she continued, "you think, Milord, that our dear tyrant Signor von Hapsburg, for example, would intervene if the Jew you mentioned found himself very elevated?"

"Are kings not bound to take an interest in one another?" the prince replied, rather surprised by that persistence.

"Oh, I share the general opinion on that matter."

"That is not to have one, Marchesa."

"But it's to have everyone's," she said.

Forsiani looked at Wilhelm, whom a part of that powerful response escaped, as he was a little young and only admiring at that moment.

"Madame, there would doubtless also be a good many Majesties shocked by the casualness of that clever man," he said, not knowing where she was trying to go.

"Let's suppose, if you don't mind, someone less Hebraic; I believe I could affirm to you that the beloved cousins of the king would then be inattentive, as the king of France, Louis XIV and his minister were inattentive when Lord Oliver set about protecting England and Charles Stuart. How many Majesties would have been shocked by the 'casualness' of that brilliant personage? You see, it's sufficient to pick one's time. Let's suppose more: here's Signor d'Anthas; the idea comes to him quite naturally to be King of Naples. Who would oppose the success of such a project undertaken in a suitable manner?"

Prince Forsiani did not reply for a moment. "Signor Strally-d'Anthas is a little young," he said, finally, as if accepting the joke.

"Would you like me to tell you a little story?" she said, leaning back with a cheerful negligence. "A prince—a prince such as Signor Strally could easily become; a domain in Italy would suffice—Prince Carlos, in Spain, was seventeen years old, the same age as the Count, and very nearly the same age as Alexander when the latter applied himself by way of distraction, to defeating the armies of the great kings of Asia and conquering the world. You won't tell me, I think, that the prince was a child? His mother, a Farnese, had given him Parma at fifteen to habituate him. One morning, he woke up with the thought about which we were talking: to be King of the Two Sicilies.[1] He imparted it to one of his friends, the Duke of Mortemart. The Duke replied, naturally, that his father would be delighted. Threading the needle, one arrives at finding in one's veins the blood of Capets, Bourbons, etc.; in lamenting the fate of the unfortunate state of Naples, the target of factions that divide it; in wanting to 'lift up that great people again . . .'

"In the end, he departs, taking a few hundred men with him. He disembarks, beats the Imperials at Bitonte like an angel, suddenly seizes the scepter and crown, has himself crowned king by Pope Clement XII and receives the investiture of the realm by the congress of Aix before anyone has time to react. You've seen that, Prince. You were attached to the Roman embassy, I believe, and knew his future minister Tannuci intimately.[2] And when

---

1 Carlos III of Spain (1716-1788) had become King of Naples and Sicily in 1734; he succeeded to the Spanish throne in 1759. The associate named erroneously by Villiers as the Duke of Mortemart (a title used by members of an influential French military dynasty) was actually the Duke of Montemar, José Carrillo de Albornoz (1671-1747), but I have left the name as Villiers renders it.

2 The name of Bernardo Tanucci is also misrendered; but I have left it as it is in the text.

Austria wanted to take back its former property, you remember the death suffered at Velletri? What enthusiasm for the young king! Women, petty peasants—what do I know?—all took up arms and got themselves killed. Those are facts. That's how Prince Carlos of Parma became Charles III of Sicily.

"However, England had an interest, as always, in installing herself in the Gulf of Naples, a military and industrial position that she will surely occupy before long; the Italian clergy, the government of the Holy Father, had passably solid reasons for negotiating with the people one of those delicate transactions that have the consequence of augmenting the Book by several millions—a deception for which I don't think Charles III was sufficiently compensated subsequently—and Naples had belonged, since Charles Quint, to the house of Austria.

"There were, therefore, it seems to me, rather grave interests, represented by three of the most expert diplomatic cabinets in Europe, to oppose that marvelous theft. Well, no; a child said to himself: 'There's a little crown that would suit me,' and you see the end, the clarity and perfection of the rout of those three powers: Rome, Austria and England.

"I could find such feats of arms, executed by very young men, on every page of history. Look, you were talking just now about Gonzalvo di Cordova, the greatest captain of the Spanish armies, a viceroy, a veteran of cunning and glory, a warrior of the Crusades, an invincible general! He was sent as a child of nineteen or twenty, and that young man—devoid of experience, as they say—won three crushing victories over the old master, one after another. You see that youth is not impossible on these occasions, Prince. I am therefore authorized to think that, before the Austrian Empire crumbles, one such, of a certain birth and a certain valor in the measure of his ambition might, overnight—my God!—assert his rights, as one says in honest terms, or as the heads of all dynasties can say . . .

"But what's the point of talking about that?" said Tullia Fabriana, suddenly changing her tone. "Kings are unruly children, very occupied regarding everything. See how silent and sage a young man Signor Strally is!"

"That proves," the prince replied, "that a Duke of Mortemart is also something. According to you, Marchesa, the complete and entire usurpation of the Kingdom of Naples would be something seriously permissible and feasible?"

"Everything is feasible, and you know very well, dear Prince, that in politics, many things are permissible, except not succeeding. But let's stop, I beg you; we have the air of conspiring, which will end up darkening the conversation," added the smiling beauty.

Ten o'clock chimed on a church that dates from the time of Charlemagne, Santa-Maria della Trinita.[1]

"*Au revoir*, dear Marchesa!" said the prince, getting up.

"You're quitting me?"

"An obligatory visit to the governor of Vecchio. After our recent words, is it not necessary for me to warn the fortress to hold hard?"

---

1 The reader will probably recall that ten o clock chimed before Forsiani and Wilhelm arrived; at Tullia's palace; Villiers probably means eleven.

"Oh, if it's for the good of the State, I forgive you," Fabriana replied. "Good evening and *bon voyage*."

They stood up.

"Who knows?" she continued. "Perhaps you'll see me again soon in Naples; the air is very pure there. *Au revoir*, then, dear Prince." And she held out her hand.

The prince kissed her fingertips amicably.

"I'm receiving tomorrow," she said, turning to Wilhelm very amiably. "I hope to see you in the evening, Count."

"Your Grace is extremely kind to me," replied the young man, bowing.

Left alone, Fabriana returned to sit down in her place. Her face had taken on an anxious and somber expression; one would not have recognized the woman of a few moments before in confrontation with that sudden transformation. After a minute, she murmured a few muffled inconsequential words, and then got to her feet and left the drawing room.

The prince and Wilhelm went downstairs. Once in the saddle, Forsiani said: "You can continue tomorrow, then, but be careful to master yourself, as you did this evening. No follies, my dear child . . . not yet, at least," he added, with a smile.

"Don't worry, Milord," Wilhelm replied.

They galloped for a while. Having arrived on the quay of the Trinity, the ambassador said: "*Au revoir*, Wilhelm. If you need your old friend, write to me in Naples."

The young man leaned toward the prince and embraced him with a spontaneous movement.

"Come on, courage!" added Prince Forsiani, in a slightly emotional voice. "Without any doubt, the most difficult part is done. Here you are in life! March!"

He shook his hand forcefully and departed toward the Via Larga.

The young man remained alone for a minute, pensive and motionless. The sky was blue, the starts bright, the orange-trees embalmed, the night was serene and warm.

"I'm young," he said, and passed his hand over his forehead.

A distant serenade reached him.

"Oh my God!" he said, with a tone of naïve and profound sadness. "Why should I not love, being alone on earth? Oh, how beautiful that woman is! How I love her already, how I am dying of love for her!"

A few moments later he spurred his horse and took the opposite route, toward San Lorenzo.

Chapter X

The Enchanted Palace

THE FABRIANI PALACE was a superb labyrinth whose meanders hid a savant order. The great Florentine architects of the fifteenth century had expended a care thereon and a magnificence of extreme planning. The Marchesa had not changed anything, or very little. The interior secrets of the palace dated back two hundred years, and alone in the world, she held Ariadne's thread.

As it was situated on high ground, far from other palaces, one could not look over the walls of the park and gardens from any other edifice. Those walls were between thirty and thirty-five feet high, and three or three-and-a-half thick. Enormous expanses of ivy, flowers and moss covered them almost entirely. The gate of the long avenue was closed by solid iron battens.

The great trees were very leafy and closely packed in the pathways. There were antique statues, a fountain with a thin silvery thread received in an alabaster urn; swans in a pond surrounded by cypresses and bordered with white marble steps; bushes of Egyptian roses, thousands of flowers of Asia and Europe with broad leaves fallen on the grass, and gracious greyhounds lying down.

And then the great silence.

The park, in the middle, was like a vast sheet of enameled grass, where roe deer and gazelles played. Something strangely Oriental emanated, in the sunlight, from those perfumes and that shade; a mysterious and profound charm flowed in the air of that solitude. Circe's gardens must have been similar.

That grandiose silence had enveloped the palace for many years. It never emerged therefrom, except for nights of fêtes, which were rare. The interior door of the gardens was sealed; one could only descend into them from Tullia's balcony.

The staff occupied the other façade, the one situated beyond the interior courtyards, which overlooked Florence. The marchesa had reserved exclusively for herself the entire façade that had a view of the gardens; the domestics never went into that part of the palace except for days of reception. Xoryl was sufficient for Fabriana.

Xoryl was the pretty child in the Greek costume glimpsed during the evening. She was a daughter of Athens once abandoned to the hazard of the streets, at the age of twelve or thirteen, by an unknown and sad family. Tullia had perceived her one day, while traveling, on the high road; the child was playing in the ruins. The marchesa appeared to examine the little girl's features with a sudden and singular attention, and, suddenly taking her into her carriage, had simply brought her back to Italy with her.

Letting that flower of poverty grow up in her palace, the latter had become charming. During the fevers caused by the change of climate and life, Fabriana had watched over her personally with a thousand cares, and if the beautiful Xoryl was not under the ground, she owed it to her mistress. She was raised and educated during the first years; the marchesa had never addressed a word of reproach or impatience to her, and the child was happy in her tranquil slavery. She allowed herself to live without loving anything except Fabriana, and would have sacrificed herself gladly if it had been necessary.

She was not her friend or her servant; she was her protégée. She scarcely had to occupy herself with a light task that the mildness of her mistress rendered facile and amiable. Was it not a pleasure for her to be of some utility? Predisposed by the features of her figure to solitary habits, Xoryl was silent and had a liking for isolation. She took pleasure in dreaming in her room, lying on the carpet with her elbow on a cushion, following the smoke of a narghile with her gaze, through her long black eyelashes, like the sultanas of seraglios. She loved to dream about the gulfs of Greece, the temples of the gods of old and her verdant pagan mountains. Humble, she still remembered her homeland, although it had only had a bitter hospitality for her childhood, and as she thought, because of the air where Tullia Fabriana respired, had also been elevated, she only recalled her homeland tranquilly in order to remember the beauty of its sky, her proud poverty, the ruins that had welcomed her childhood, the glory of the warriors dead in ancient times, and its lost liberty.

Thus Xoryl lived, faithful and taciturn.

Sometimes, she was given pearls, diamonds or sequin bracelets, while Tullia said to her in the soft language of Athens, after a kiss on the forehead: "You're free to quit me, Xoryl; will you remember me when you're in your homeland?" At which Xoryl smiled, without responding, looking at her naïvely with moist eyes.

The black cashmere fez whose gold tassel undulated over her shoulder, with the rest of the Oriental costume, cast a kind of natal charm over her lovely physiognomy. She appeared to receive the shade and light of Fabriana's beauty when she stood before her, and then she went away with what she had been given.

That young woman therefore sufficed for Fabriana when she wanted to maintain herself in a profound and absolute retreat; and it was by means of such simple details that she had succeeded in dominating that retreat completely and getting her bearings in the immense palace.

The great staircase of honor that led to the three different floors of the palace divided on the landing of the first floor, thanks to a winged partition circled with strips of bronze that deployed at will and were barred internally. The other service stairways leading to the floors of that façade from the gardens had been walled up.

The intervals of the colonnades of the ground floor that bordered the gardens were filled in by potted orange trees, behind which there was nothing but a thick marble-clad wall devoid of windows.

The uppermost floor appeared to be composed of servants' bedrooms. It was nothing of the sort. Its casements were those of a narrow corridor without issues. Behind the corridor wall were the real chambers overlooking the interior courtyards; no one lived in them.

It was impossible to reach the roofs of that façade. A long gap in continuity separated them from other terraces. They were formed of tiles disposed in angles, without any kind of border or point of support.

Thus, the partition of the staircase once established, the entire façade, with its three floors overlooking the gardens, was isolated from the exterior and the interior. There was a kind of sudden desert. Unless one had penetrated into one of the chambers or one of the drawing rooms of the first floor, plunging into the bronze circles of the partition, it would have been radically chimerical to claim to know what was happening there, since it was possible to reach the upper floors without passing via the first.

But throughout the extent of that first floor, all the doors of the apartments had a steel wire hidden in the woodwork, in such a fashion that the most distant door, suddenly opened by a visitor, would have caused a bell to ring in Xoryl's room, which was two rooms away from the one where the marchesa slept. If, after an express prohibition of entering those apartments, the bolts being shot, a lackey, a steward, a majordomo or any other diurnal or nocturnal individual had taken it into his head, curiously, to come and force the doors—whether to steal, to spy, to abduct, to rape or to murder; what other design is possible?—the pretty child would have extended her hand toward two steel buttons hidden in the wall, and without disturbing herself otherwise, would have precipitated the intruder into a sixty-foot oubliette, which was the partial content of the window-less walls of the ground floor, even if he were at the other extremity of the façade.

A band of a dozen individuals would not have necessitated more expense, for the parquet suddenly opened up over an extent of several meters under all the doors at the same time.

The furniture was arranged in a certain manner expressly to avoid any disorder.

The thing, in itself, cast a shadow of death and shock over the Asiatic splendor of the long laminated drapes, the gilt, the mirrors and the paintings, the chandeliers and the statues that decorated the large sumptuous rooms. The constructions on the triple row of beams welded with iron appeared abruptly under the chandeliers in the walls of the opening; once fallen there, it was the end. Tullia did not intend that the secret should be known. Obliged to choose between a blow from above and low justice, and the imprudent eventuality of a lack of success in what she had resolved to accomplish—which she would effectively have been risking, in addition to her personal security, by allowing the curious to leave alive—she left matters to fatality.

"You will strike, and thus fulfill my will," she had said to Xoryl one evening. And, taking her by the hand, she had guided her by the light of a torch through the maze of those lost cells; she had taken her down to the deepest of the subterrains and there, somber and sad, she had shown her what to do on such an occasion. It was simple. Darts dipped in deadly poisons . . . the night . . . a masked door . . . the gardens . . . one of the crates of lime of which there was a great reserve under the flagstones, etc. . . . . would have caused the traces of whoever presented themselves to disappear forever.

Xoryl had inclined her amiable brunette head, murmuring in an excessively muted voice the Oriental formula: "To hear is to obey."

"That's good," Tullia Fabriana had said to her, not without a gaze that had gone to read the child's soul and come back satisfied.

Xoryl would, therefore, have carried out that task conscientiously without even waking Tullia if she happened to be asleep at the time. The murder and annihilation of the victim would not have lasted as long as the song of a nightingale in the foliage. The phases of the drama were foreseen almost to the minute. The echo of it would not have penetrated the black velvet curtains brocaded with gold whose fabric was amassed on each side of the interior doors. The execution terminated, the child would have activated the powerful springs again, and the replaced parquets would have reconnected the incisions in the flagstones or carpets, adapting themselves thereto invisibly.

Alternatively, if the invader appeared to be of a certain caste, he could be left dead in the gardens. The height of the windows would have justified the fractures occasioned by the fall into the oubliette, etc. An accident that no one had the right to delve into responded to any question.

At the other extremity of the park there was a pavilion backed up against the great wall, and one could enter or exit via that pavilion unknown to the staff. It opened to the country on the bank of the Arno, almost always deserted at that location. A telescope permitted the surroundings to be explored and time to be taken if it were thought to be utterly indispensable that such entrances and exits be unobserved.

Tullia Fabriana, forced, not only for herself—if it had only been a matter of herself, she would doubtless not have employed so many measures—to contend with all kinds of human instincts, took very seriously the precautions that ought to defend her and ensure the success of what she had charged her will to realign sooner or later. Passers-by, with very few exceptions, have no other joy in this life than trying to harm superior individuals and outraging indifferently in their speech those whose imperfections they believe that they remark.

Thus, by virtue of respect for the human form, she tried as much as possible to spare them the trouble of that malice in her regard. Her procedures constituted a talisman more reliable than the ring of the Lydian magus. They attained in their detail, as will be seen, vertiginous proportions of lucidity and profundity. It was as strong and clear as algebra. There are no true measures except for those taken fully—which is to say, those at the exact height of those against whom they are taken. Fabriana, knowing the consequences and disasters virtually contained in the smile of a valet "who thinks he sees something suspicious" and who is on the alert to profit from a forgetfulness, conceived human weakness very well, pardoned it and found a thousand excusable reasons for it, but did not want to be the victim of it.

A stone stairway led internally to the platform of the walls that surrounded the gardens. At night, two enormous mountain dogs, mastiffs trained for that work, roamed that platform and would have deterred anyone who, by chance, for whatever reason, had judged it appropriate to set a ladder against it. Their barking, in any case, would have given warning of the attempt; at a strike of Xoryl's bell, half a dozen gigantic negroes, armed to the teeth, would have rushed silently into the surrounding area.

And then, from Xoryl's window, the gaze embraced the summit of the walls. The charming savage had an eagle eye and was a divinely accurate shot; without having need of the negroes she would have unmasked a lamp with a reflective projector and illuminated the platforms with a circular sweep in a flash. Then, seizing a small carbine—a jewel of a weapon with an ebony butt encrusted with ornaments and precious arabesques, a miracle of precision of which the marchesa had made her a present—she would have fired immediately at the first malevolent head that appeared.

Fabriana's private cutlery, cups and plates were gold, and Xoryl wiped them attentively, with a very fine cloth, after the domestics. The two cooks had been in the palace for many years, and they bought what was necessary themselves, with the greatest discernment, unaided, except on days of reception. There was only one maître d'hôtel, an old man, very tranquil and very attached to the palace; he had served Duke Fabriano, the marchesa's father, who had died poisoned, as has been said. The old man had the responsibility of the sommelier, not long dead. Alone, with one of the negroes, he had the right to speak to Xoryl and to warn her of what was coming from outside.

In the morning and the evening he set a magnificent table incrusted with strips of ivory and nacre, in a vestibule on the ground floor, opening to one of the interior courtyards. The cooks brought him what was necessary, one after another, and he had orders never to quit the vestibule when he had commenced his task and never to let any domestic enter it under any pretext whatsoever. Once the table was set, he waited for Xoryl to ring and, pressing a spring adapted to four bronze chains, the table rose up of its own accord, silently, in grooves; the parquet of the floor above parted, and allowed it to pass through.

With the aid of those precautions, it would have been very difficult to mix opium or any other poison with the wine or the food. Xoryl had the custom, by virtue of an excess of prudence, of testing the appetite of the two mastiffs before Tullia sat down at table; that was known, and was one advantage more.

It is necessary to remember that there cannot be anything petty in the ensemble of a divine plan, that every detail takes its value from the general conception and that a truly profound mind clothes items of the slightest appearances with their veritable viewpoint. Reading the history of conspiracies that fell, with the heads of the conspirators, one is not astonished to see, not how they fell—that is of no importance, except in schools to exercise the memory of young and amiable children—but why they fell. In discovering the true reason for their collapse into the void, a thinking mind remains positively nonplussed. It is in the forgetfulness of a miserable detail that great Fatality[1] goes to take refuge in its entirety. Is it possible, therefore, that the most intrepid geniuses of revolt, whose gaze embraces, without disturbance, the developments of a formidable machination, are resigned to repeat the odious diction of the vulgar: "One can't foresee everything."

It was for that reason that Tullia Fabriana took account of trivia: because of great Fatality.

For her, as she was not enslaved by any habit, as she had accustomed her body early to hunger, vigils, cold and fatigue, privations were natural, those things even pushed to alarming proportions, would have been blunted against her beauty as if sliding over the iron constitution of a Sergius.[2]

She doubtless only counted that beauty, truly marvelous moreover, as one weapon more; and it is well-known that in Italy, particularly in Tuscany, the beauty of women commonly lasts much longer than in other countries. It is a recognized fact, it appears, albeit rather bizarre, that the most beautiful women in Tuscany are not those twenty years old but those who have often passed forty. That circumstance, be it said in passing, could not be unfavorable to her projects.

The concise notes and unknown formulae that the three alchemical researchers had left in their laboratory

---

1 Author's note: "Fatality is taken here in the sense of an unfortunate concordance, the force of circumstances, and not from any other point of view."
2 Probably the fourth century martyr, Saint Sergius., whose legend depicts him robust in resisting torture..

had smoothed out the difficulties of the science of poisons for her. Like Locusta, she was consummate in the art of preparations that devastate but without leaving any trace. The strangest Florentine and Indian poisons were manipulated familiarly by her and she often devoted long hours to studying them and investigating their potency.

To rediscover subtle and penetrating compositions with the aid of which the mere emanation of a piece of paper is mortal had not been difficult for her. She had some whose effects were slow enough for no suspicion to arise, and which only struck after an interval of three or four slumbers, for example. The employment of letters as a means is nevertheless essentially difficult, firstly because of the care and exactitude that the preparation requires, and then because of the precautions taken by sovereigns and pontiffs to escape those sorts of attempts. However, are there not always letters that princes take care to read? It is only a matter of finding two initial lines gripping in regard to their most intimate desire of the moment, something that the habitude of courts, the science of society, observation, etc., facilitates greatly at a certain social rank. It would not have been difficult for her to design the armories of some ambassador or consulate, to melt a seal—in brief, to send a letter in such a manner that, even supposing, improbably, the failure of the attempt, it would have been impossible to know whence it came.

Now, for example, suppose two or three words in an important passage, written in a manner difficult to read, necessitating the approach of the eyes; a phrase whose meaning is dubious and of great interest, so that a person listening to it is led to seize the paper, inadvertently from his secretary's hands in order to check the matter himself and justify the superiority of his own eyes, etc., etc.—a letter, in sum containing words more fit for the lighted fire than the archives—we say letter, although we could also think about a flower, a fan or a handkerchief . . .

Remember the latter part of the Middle Ages in Italy.

It was therefore possible to affirm that, thanks to her exceptional position, Tullia Fabriana held, in a thousand forms, the life and death of almost all the crowned heads of Europe in the palm of her beautiful hand. Is not Death, in a mask of white velvet or pink satin, still Death? That did not raise the shadow of a doubt for her.

In the marchesa's bedroom there was something special. An admirably welded door rotating on itself with a section of the wall revealed a flight of stone steps, which led to a profound subterrain.

That subterrain had no issue of its own. It penetrated under the palace for the full extent of the façade. There was nothing there but iron barrels painted the color of wood, arranged one beside another. It resembled a large wine-cellar, except that a lead tube linked all the barrels together and rose up in serpentine spirals through the stones. Only Fabriana knew what terrifying extremity was contained there.

At the entrance to the subterrain, on the third step, there was another invisible door, similarly closed by a section of the wall that moved when one pressed a steel button the color of stone hidden in the moss.

In that second subterrain there was a torch, a mirror, a crate of disguises and their security papers, excellent double pistols, accompanied by two traveling épées and two poisoned yatagans. Two purses of gold mingled with diamonds were dropped on top of the crate.

In case of a surprise and an arrest by an escort—something that seemed beyond normal expectations, but with which she was ready to deal—she would have taken Xoryl in her arms, for fear that, not knowing the dangerous steps, the child might have fallen there as into a precipice and been killed. Once descended, the wall closing on them was thick enough and sufficiently perfectly joined for no sound or other indication to betray them. In any case, there was the first door to find before reaching that one. The depths of the subterrain coiled around, it was as difficult as the hypogea or serapea of Egypt. They would disguise themselves and wait for nightfall. It opened, by means of a hidden door like the others, on to the Arno; a boat suspended at the entrance above the river only had need of a swing accompanied by the sweep of a yatagan through the ropes to be set afloat, and they would row away.

Fabriana knew where to find African horses, a league away. Once in the saddle they would go to Venice or Genoa; the marchesa had two pleasure villas there, and security.

The essential thing had been to attain that goal, to be unapproachable, invisible and impregnable, in good conditions or in spite of everything; and to be able to get away, whenever she wanted, from the heart of Florence in broad daylight.

However, the palace resembled other palaces; apart from the grandeur and the beauty of the architecture, it presented nothing particular. Busy lackeys and stewards circulated in the exterior courtyards and apartments; but there was little noise. The distinctive character of the palace was a certain silence.

Visits were frequent and agreeably received; the conversation there had an engaging liberty; one might have thought that the doors opened by themselves and that negligence was even pushed to excess. At the slightest anxiety, however, the course of things could change its appearance instantaneously and was deformed as far as becoming terrible. In three seconds, it would have taken on the appearance of a state of siege with a precision and an intensity of deployment of all its force at once, which would have crushed, without any tumult or disorder, those who were there with evil intent, in the gears of the living stones. Fatality would have obeyed mechanically, in a very horrible manner. As in Arabian tales, there would have been a disappearance. Bursts of laughter would have been annihilated by laughter in the darkness if, by chance there had been jokers among the victims of the somber moment. After the lightning, everything would have reentered the habitual tranquility, including the smile of the pale enchantress.

Of that state of things, the result was that Marchesa Fabriana could do almost anything she wished in her home, without being seen, spied upon, suspected or commented upon; as much as possible, she was not at anyone's mercy, and could deem herself sheltered from the perpetual uncertainties of being troubled in her solitude.

We will add that those precautions, had they been remarked in part, would have seemed quite natural on the part of two women living alone, retired and exposed. The isolated situation of the palace would have been sufficient to justify it.

Chapter XI

Chivalrous Adventures

Ye shall know them by their fruits.[1]

IT was by the little door of the pavilion that Tullia
Fabriana often went out by night dressed as a cavalier,
an épée at her hip and a mask on her face.

Always alone.

Under her garments she wore a steel breastplate of
unparalleled lightness; it was the work of one of the old
artists of the sixteenth century who once produced masterpieces of armor and sculpture. One of those unknown
men, who steeped damascened lace, had also made the
fine and powerful coat of mail that imprisoned her from
the feet to the throat.

Her gauntlets were woven from fine steel thread,
marvelously hidden under silk. Her fur hat, from which
false curls of black hair escaped, had an interior visor
that she could raise or lower as she pleased

---

1 *Matthew* 7:16.

She did not seem at all hindered in that costume; she walked quickly, her cloak thrown over her shoulder, like a knight. In spite of her modest appearance, the rare passers-by almost always stood aside from her path, without knowing why.

What did that clothing signify? Was it the love of adventures? No; she was not a woman to commit those follies.

The familiar cries of the birds of death said to her:

"Beautiful lady, there is the midnight knell. It's the hour when we have bumped our wings against your windows; we know your lamp. The streets are deserted, the sword breaks in the ambush; it's black danger that is lying in wait, with our eyes, in the sleeping solitude. Woman you are becoming reckless, you who are always so prudent, so profound and so sage. Turn back! That is an old man's advice; we are interested in you."

She walked on, advancing tranquilly through back streets in equivocal and tenebrous outlying districts.

Oh, it was because she sometimes experienced the great vertigo of self; she felt it deeply: what remained human might quit her at any moment; she was almost no longer earthbound, and did not exist in truth. It was necessary that she remembered her body, though, since she had said: "I'll wait."

That is why, by a necessary reaction, she came to steep herself in the spectacle of some suffering, in order not to forget that she existed.

Masculine costume had appeared to her to be more comfortable than feminine costume in the circumstance; that was the motive that had determined her choice.

She climbed many disgusting stairways, she found a good number of horrible scenes; her handkerchief impregnated with odorous salts barely preserved her from suffocating in noxious atmospheres.

She gave her gold and her science, not because it was a "good deed" but because she might as well do that as anything else, and she had the opportunity. Without a doubt she knew the irremediable immensity of dolors too well to think for a minute that even if she appeared to millions of individuals in Europe alone it would have signified very much, so the question of the good that she did was only very accessory for her. Such fantasies would probably have been displaced if they had been dictated solely by a motive of an inferior order.

The immense forgetfulness of everything, of her rank, her position, the conventions of feminine clothing, and the conversations and salutations to which persons of distinction devoted themselves in order to kill time, enveloped those steps. An aureole of eternity illuminated her in all those strange fashions. She often spent the night like that, at the risk of being assassinated, coming back at daybreak without having taken off her mask, without having spoken her name and without having allowed her gloves to get wet. Comprehend her who can!

"That's good," she said, and she left.

Cain's wife would have understood. She lacked the "sensitivity" that charitably-speaking people like to find in woman.

Cold, she could have an infinite sorrow within her; but those sick children, for example, who held out their little arms with suppliant inflections of their voices did not move that somber, inaccessible heart very much.

The persons mentioned would have been moved, making speeches two hours later on "human nature," on seeing the poor cured children either martyrizing some animal, insulting some unfortunate or committing some act of deep, cowardly, stubborn malevolence with neither a goal nor a voice—in brief, lacking charity for everything suffering as they had suffered. The speech would have lasted several half-hours, a loss of time that she avoided by not being sterilely impressed. She acted in the measure of the forces at her disposal; little as it was, it was what she had been permitted to do. Was it her fault, then, if even dolors could not trouble her heart?

She had accepted to fill that mysterious métier in Florence, in spite of the two shelters she had also established in Tuscany under a name other than her own. She seemed to have created the original pastime in order to suppress something, however trivial, in universal misfortune. Her constancy, on that subject, was never discouraged or disgusted by the occasion. It was a fashion of waiting for that for which she was waiting.

Her hand did not tremble any more in holding a scalpel than a book or a sword, and it doubtless appeared as natural to her to write next to a wretched mattress the formula for strange drugs that relieve torments as to write an ode in Sapphic verse on the inconstancy of the passions

In this, Tullia Fabriana did not cease to be great and impassive.

It was not necessary for her to reflect, to decide upon the risks and perils of disguises; it was that she had to do what seemed good to her, without disturbing anyone.

The first time that, in front of her mirror, as she dressed, the steel mail had glittered over her white and supple limbs, she had a sad smile. The second time, she did not even pay attention.

She had seen herself forced to act alone doubtless because she was not bound to any known being, and, when she consented to action, she had to love and do everything, however trivial it was, exactly as well as was permitted to her.

The colossal, stunning, extraterrestrial science, the intuitive skill of her hand and her cold gaze of genius could not be replaced; a few lines written in haste on her knees, wounds closed and limbs saved, the withering and desolation of many existences warded off by a moment of her good will and courage, were preferable to the insufficiency of some money and worth as much as another occupation.

In any case, the perpetual concentration of her thought within herself permitted her to labor anywhere, doing no matter what, as well as in her palace.

One or two words spoken by her absolute and tranquil voice gave more strength and calmed more—touching more accurately, in sum, in view of the security of her intellectual evaluation of those she approached—than the exhortations of those who always have the mania of "being in the right" would have done.

Let it be said in passing that sensible hearts, simple and direct hearts, are often only good for making those in whom they take an interest suffer; with the best will, they are generally the cause of greater embarrassment.

In sum, she was able, as a woman, to deem her action to be a kind of duty, and she fulfilled that duty stoically.

Often, when she came home in the morning, at the hour when the light of the lamps was fading, when the sky was covered in mortuary tints, when the weariness of the spirit and the disgust of the heart left nothing but emptiness, an immense and heavy emptiness, in the discouragement of thought—at the time, in sum, when majority of people understand the possibility of eternal oblivion—yes, often, she heard the last measures of final dances sounding, muffled, through the blinds and orange-groves of other palaces. But she did not waste time recalling, then, the hours of black dreams and profound stupors that she had just quit. She did not compare the panicked agonies and nameless cries, the howls and puerile thirst for vengeance—in sum, the varied concerts of plaints that the amateurs of repugnant Poverty present, when it is not silent; which is to say, even more lugubrious—with the gusts of harmonious and insouciant joy.

She did not judge, having other thoughts.

She lavished her strength and her aid, because it suited her. What the brilliant elect of nocturnal fêtes did and what she had spent the night accomplishing were equivalent for her. Everyone had done their duty and used their time in some manner, and in accordance with their preference.

Three times, in the five or six years that she had been risking those excursions, when she was in Florence in the intervals of her distant voyages, Tullia Fabriana had been attacked.

The first time she had held firm, without calling for help, against paupers, and thanks to her flamboyant manner of handling a sword, they had fled after a few thrusts with the point, which left three of her assailants on the pavement.

The second time she had thrown a handful of florins and said to them in a calm voice: "That's because I don't want to kill you."

And, opening her cloak, the marchesa allowed the sight of the loaded pistols in her belt.

The third time she found herself suddenly surrounded. It was two o'clock in the morning, as she emerged from a hovel where she had just saved two moribund families from malady and hunger.

She lowered her visor precipitately, fired two shots and drew her sword. As she was dealing with a drunken mob of paupers, who rushed her blindly, any defense was paralyzed and impossible; they threw themselves on her arms. She freed herself for a second time with a terrible movement, but, finding herself disarmed, she had a bitter smile under her helm. A stiletto had just broken its point on her breastplate, another would have blinded her but for her visor; in spite of the punches she plunged, with precision and a strange force, for several seconds, into a number of bloated faces and breasts, she understood immediately that she would end up being stifled or strangled. At the height of the struggle large cutlasses were seen gleaming; she had already borne a poisoned ring to her lips in order not to fall at their mercy alive, when one of the individuals called an unknown name, which she did not even hear.

At that single word, they all drew apart. A few words were exchanged in low voices; their effect was astonishing. Those who surrounded her knelt before her and begged pardon. She made no reply, but, standing in the midst of hideous groups illuminated by the lantern of an ex-voto, she replaced her sword in its sheath and drew away slowly.

After that, no one bothered her again. In the most deserted and darkest back streets, an appeal of her voice would have sufficed to defend her, but she would not have appealed. Tacitly, the poor had an understanding to recognize her and not to do her any harm. They refrained from following her out of respect; in any case, a saddled horse awaited her at daybreak in some location, and a time of gallop would have distanced her from spies of any sort; there was never any question of it . . .

Chapter XII

Fiat nox[1]

"Fortunate is he who lives and dies without
a wife and children!"
(Augustus Caesar.)

THE day after the presentation of the Count of
Strally, at about eight o'clock in the evening, Tulia
Fabriana was in her palace, in a spacious and remote
apartment. It was the one she preferred; she spent the
greater part of her time in Florence there; no one other
than Xoryl had ever penetrated it. The circular drawing
room presented an aspect of extraordinary splendors.
Eight great statues in black basalt extracted from the
tumulary valleys of Ethiopia, the naïvely sculpted heads
of which expressed and interior torment, supported together, with their sixteen extended and tensed arms, the
fresco of the ceiling representing veiled Isis in a night
full of stars. The hangings were replaced by overlap-

---

1 "Let there be night."

ping draperies in yellow velvet with golden reflections. A profusion of skins of Levantine lions and tigers hid the parquet completely. A unique casement, of precious stained glass was open over the gardens. Ropes woven of golden loops and filigrees retained there, half-extended, a mat of brown straw, providing protection from the sun without too much obscurity.

Near the balustrade there were two nacre boxes filled with all kinds of rare flowers from the most distant climates. Sheaves of ancient weapons were appliquéd in the draperies.

In the middle of the room, on an ebony table, a golden Florentine vase was resplendent, a bowl full of fruits and two enameled cups of great antiquity. A sphinx of colossal length, similarly in solidified black lava, making a kind of pendant for the caryatids, was placed in a secant drawn to the left of the casement. Its enormous back was hollowed out and filled with pelts of marten and ermine. On that magnificent bed of repose, Fabriana was lying indolently that evening. Next to her, a blue night-light, raised on a golden tripod and lit night and day in a little crystal urn, was burning an odorous oil.

To the extent that it was possible to judge, the marchesa was very tall and svelte. Because of the stifling heat she was dressed in a cloud of batiste in the form of a peignoir, cleft at the breast and uncovering her shoulders slightly. There were droplets of diamante sweat on her firm and snowy flesh. The transparent and soft weave that enveloped her body allowed the plenitudes of the statue of Cleomenes to be divined.[1] Her head, on which the radiance of the night-light fell, had a very white complexion. The heavy golden tresses of her hair were divided over her beautiful mat forehead and fell down in fleeces of radiant curls behind her head, inundating her neck and her back. Her eyes, in which the drowned gleams of the pupils sparkled like two black stones, were gazing vaguely at the terrible group enchained around her. She had eyebrows of an intelligent impassivity. The nose, traced with a severe delicacy of design, was straight; the expression of her face was seductive; her agile nostrils were mobile, rosy and diaphanous.

Life was circulating with a healthy sensuality in that beautiful recumbent lady. Her perfect mouth was bright red, as if velveted by the creases of its beautiful skin; her milky teeth were biting her lower lips slightly. Yesterday, the smile had tempered the regally disdainful expression of that mouth; today, nothing was smiling in her physiognomy.

One of her arms was curbed over her forehead in an abandoned attitude; between two fingers of the hand that hung over that forehead she was holding the bud of an Indian flower, a kind of brunella with excessive perfumes, which she stirred, graciously touching her face with it from time to time. Her other arm, molded by some divine sculptor, fell from the sleeve of floating lace and dangled all the way to the furs. On one of the slender fingers of that hand she had a gold ring constellated

---

1 This reference is enigmatic; no known work by the sculptor Cleomenes, mentioned by Pliny the Elder, survives.

with large emeralds; that ring was her only adornment; she never took it off, even when sleeping, for particular reasons. Her bare feet were playing in white velvet mules festooned with Moorish embroideries.

She was dreaming thus, lost in the midst of the beauty, emerging, suavely lying down, from the somber background that surrounded her; and certainly, to see her so nearly positively exempt from possible worries, one could not have divined the nature of the terrifying dream, the unusual dream, that was alive in her unexplored soul!

She gazed for a long time at the immeasurable torsos on which the light of the night-light was mirrored.

Outside, the evening was darkening.

Often, in the country, a ray of moonlight embracing ruins is an evocation. Stones clad in moss and memories appear to have seen so much history and forgotten events. Legends awake, the woods and the heaths are populated with visions and murmurs, forms that wander in the silence. Then, like the scientist who reconstructs the fossils of the night of the world from a fragment of a tusk, the soul recreates temples, manors and palaces with the debris of a column, and, meditation touching the vast dream of existence, the great melancholy of Becoming envelops the mind invincibly.

Here, in this room, the entourage of caryatids seemed to exclude the savage majesty of it; they lacked the immensity, the spectacle of space set ablaze by the simoom. They appeared no longer to be surrounded by the solitude of the centuries . . . but they bore all that with them for Fabriana. Her soul substituted deserts for those ruins. At her will, the chamber became profound; under her gaze, the walls recoiled and became distant. Those black colossi, snatched from the tombs of the kings of Abyssinia and Egypt, awoke ancient deeds within them. One might often have thought that their eyes gave the impression of exchanging a nameless, limitless, hopeless thought with her eyes, icy like them, sad with their sorrow.

For a long time, they had had no one but the pilgrims of the banks of the Nile at whom to cast at intervals one of those reflections that their silence guarded and their silence inspired. From what sovereign had Fabriana's ancestors purchased them? She did not know. But she loved those dolorous faces, doubtless because they symbolized something for her.

She lowered her eyelids and, as if prey to mental concentrations focused on a single viewpoint, murmured the single phrase: "I'll try."

A few moments went by.

"In any case," murmured the superb dreamer, "is it not the only reality for which it is worth the trouble of living, now?"

Her gaze was raised again toward the old black stones with human faces, which seemed to stand for something in the depths of her thought, and she continued speaking in a calm and pure voice, although very soft and scarcely distinct.

"Let's try to recall things and phantoms, since I'm going to live! Yes, the evening when, on the leaden waves of the Nile, deafened by the noise of the oars of the imperial boat, when their air was impregnated with scents exhaled by the immense efflorescences that Nubian slaves planted around the valley of the tombs, and on the high pyramids silvered by Oriental nights, the inscriptions of the magi of Osiris shone like the beacons of the desert; when caravans laden with myrrh, gum, camphor and gold coming from Bactriana or Persia passed confusedly in the distance, in the expanse, with their torches, their elephants, their riches and their slaves; when, through a mirage of sands, verdure and stars, the wind was embalmed in the foliage of cedars and palm trees; when the immortal phoenixes flew over the sepulchers of the pharaohs; in sum, when the world was rich for once in its life, often, as soon as night fell, the beautiful queen of the ancient Heptanomide loved to linger over the river.

"Then, from the pillars of Hercules to the boreal steppes, the world, with its peoples, its kings and its mystery, came to that woman!

"Her name formulated all those images."

She remained speechless for a minute, leaning her elbow on the sphinx.

"She was, I believe, the last child of the three-hundred-year-old dynasty of the Lagide Ptolemies.[1] She descended from the Macedonian soldier cast up there by the funereal indifference of Alexander. Excess had attenuated in her the purity of the lines of that Greek beauty transmitted to her race by the soldier.

"However, thanks to the balsamic philters and the dangerous essences that the priests distilled for her, she conserved her amber and solar pallor.

---

1 i.e. Cleopatra.

"Oh, she was the great insensible! She leaned on her favorite panther in the bottom of the cange; the reeds were noisy, obstructed by alligators and hippopotami. She reposed, clad in her astral nudity, on fabrics the secrets of whose weaving have never been recovered, which were the presents of the satraps of Asia Minor. Like the Assyrian monarch, she had to prove, at an interval of eight hundred years, that death was for her only a slave like the others. The triumvir of Actium ought not to ornament his triumph with her alive! Weary of having studied lasciviously in the subterranean halls of her palace what slaves could support of torments without dying, she reflected. Playing at her feet was one of her naïve daughters raised by her to serve in a certain fashion and whom she accommodated. The vertigo of dazzling and profound nights surrounded his queen, the daughter of terrors, silence and lust! She was lost, undazzled by her own majesty, in some dream that no one would ever fathom . . .

"She was sublime."

Tullia Fabriana curbed her head, and after a second she said, like a murmur: "O past . . . !"

Those words had rendered the chamber fantastic.

"You are faithful and you guard the secrets in spite of the years without number, statues with mouths of stone! But when you sustained the trusses where the remains of those kings of old worlds reposed, embalmed, beside the Nile, you doubtless saw the great queen pass by like that!"

She gazed at them and resumed her reverie.

"O beautiful and somber friend, I do not know your story, and yet, when I heard your name pronounced for the first time, I remember having shivered, I who can no longer shiver. My soul had already revolted at the idea of being forced to live in these centuries of humiliation. As soon as my youth, in considering humankind, I understood the tears of Xerxes and, like old men, I was already only living in the past, that spectacle having hollowed out in my heart the wrinkles that age alone refused my forehead. My soul is not of these bitter times! You know that, Spirits, you who are attentive to those who speak to you without astonishment, you know that to the stories of all that history it seemed to me—more than once—that my memory, suddenly sunk in the profound domains of dream, experienced inconceivable remembrances.

"Since that time," she continued, after a silence, "since the time when I fixed my future, I have taken account, involuntarily, of the muted hesitation of my consciousness, and I try in vain to fill in long intervals. My days are welded to one another like the links of a chain that I am obliged to bear and which crushes me beneath its weight. It seems to me that for a long time my soul has stopped abruptly in the middle of I know not what immense route, and the earth appears to me as lugubrious as a prison. Oh, it's that, it's that above all that confounds me! I suffer from living, having nothing more to draw from the earth, and yet being unable to detach myself from it."

She closed her eyes during a moment of silence.

Chapter XIII

Darkness

A torch does not illuminate its base.
(Arabic proverb.)

S OMBERLY, she continued:
"I could detach myself from it! Do I not have the talisman of liberty, the ring that contains for me the night in which no one any longer toils?"

And, interrupting herself, she caused a spring in her ring to move: an emerald shifted, allowing the sight of a few grains of brown powder inside the bezel.

"But the most contrary spectacles can neither distract nor trouble me; I have no need of the ring; I have reached, by dint of struggle, my own identity. For the empire of the heavens, I would not be able to forget the supreme sadness of living nor descend from the sphere that I have attained. The sympathies and aversions of people pass indifferently before my solitude. I began to die a long time ago; the horizon has darkened; my heart is a great icy melancholy; it seems to me that I am no longer changing.

"I do not shudder because I do not love anything, and it is because I no longer cling to anything that I am above most suffering. I cannot satisfy myself with that which does not last; I have no enthusiasm for that which finishes; I do not love the noise of the wind in a forest; I do not love the ocean or the nocturnal stars; I scarcely care about a beauty that must be annulled of its own accord and is at the mercy of the passing moment; nothing terrestrial can captivate me henceforth."

As she pronounced those words, Tullia Fabriana had got up and had lit a candelabrum. She marched toward a corner of the room facing her and lifted the curtain that masked the corner. One of the cedar panels slid in the woodwork; the marchesa took a book from the covert and, placing the candelabrum on a table, she came to resume her pose on the sphinx.

She opened the volume and leafed through the pages.

There were about five hundred leaves of parchment bound between two plates of solid black metal; the fastening of the clasp was enriched with precious stones; it was a manuscript, although the evenness of the characters seemed to have a typographic perfection.

The writing was precise, delicate and compact; no erasures. Only two-thirds of the book was filled.

"However," she continued, "In spite of the scant interest I accord them, it's necessary that I remember many things, for if the secret of commencements is not unknown to me, if I have reached the crux of the mystery, if Necessity has revealed itself in me, I am no less its victim, and I ought to struggle against it to my last sigh."

She began to read silently.

This is what was written on the page:

> *Note 112. Return from the exploration in Bessarabia.*
>
> *I came to Kitta. I brought back under my breastplate the strip of stellar numbers classified on the Hermetic shelf between the Cabire signs and the tables of Eleusis, title 21.*
>
> *On the way, the Bohemians, under whose tent I had slept, explained to me the secrets of their augural science. One of the daughters of the tribe made me a present of the asbestos amulet that illuminates precipices and caverns without catching fire. The thin roll of my belt contained a rich herbal. Those women, who speak in low voices in the desert had collected them personally and dried the precious flowers; I knew the virtue of each of the plants. One evening, the third after that encounter, as I quit them, the child who had deprived herself for me of her magic stone, and to whom I had given a gold necklace, accompanied me for a few moments. She led my horse; it was dark.*
>
> *"You are as silent as the sand," she said to me, with the sound of a familiar voice. "For myself, I read the future, like all those who wander with no homeland; give me your hand, you'll see."*

That assertion made me smile; I took off
one of my gloves and, because of the obscurity,
I held above the open hand that I presented to
her the amulet that illuminates the abysms.
At the first symptom of shock that appeared
on her features—doubtless at the sight of
the sign of Isis at the summit of the mount
of Saturn as well as the constellated powers
that cover the finger of Hermes and the entire
percussion of my hand—I extended the hand
toward her. The child's eyelids fluttered; she
fell unconscious on the grass. I took the reins
again and disappeared in the darkness.

Tullia Fabriana stopped; then she murmured vaguely:
"That journey acquainted me with a battlefield,
which I might remember one day."
She resumed reading.

Some time afterwards—I do not know
under what parallels of Asia I found myself
when this happened—I had surpassed the
mountains and on a clear Oriental night I
was in a profound and silent forest. I was
looking at the Southern Cross through the
branches periodically in order to continue my
journey toward Persia or Syria.
Lost in thought, I observed a fixed point of
the Notion that I had already reached. I was
meditating on the correspondence between the
Universal, the Particular and the Individual

with Identity, Difference and the Reason for Being, presupposed and reconstituted in me by Mentality. I was plunged in visionary Abstraction and, gripped by the Immensity, I did not perceive the threat by which I was menaced. The horse bolted, abruptly alarmed either by the distant roar of a tiger or a noise of scales in the grass, and, head down, in the vertigo of its surge it drew me with its furious course into the midst of invisible dangers and I know now what imminent death.

For an instant, the night held me. The teeth of wild beasts or the coils of serpents seduced me, as well as some other malady. Death did not surprise me; here or elsewhere, it mattered little to me. At this hour rather than that, under the ocean, under foliage or underground, that had become indifferent to me. If one desire remained to me, it was to reconstruct things entirely before quitting them, but I did not even care about that, knowing that I already contained, virtually, their absolute explanation. However, I had told the Spirits that I would wait, and I did not want to accept death. I immediately recollected the Science of Fire and I calculated my forces of enchantment.

Having around me, in the ether, the virtues of chastity, having six days of fasting behind my words, having endured thirst during those six days and having bathed the pre-

vious evening, my hand traced in the air, at all hazard, the signs agreed long ago between the living and the dead. The horse stopped, described a circle and collapsed in the middle of an immense luminous clearing. I folded my arms, standing up with my eyes fixed on the night; I pronounced, singing, the great words of the Incantation, certain that I was about to be extracted from peril by something unexpected.

In fact, in front of me, in the distance, I saw a vast elephant appear; it was running. When it had arrived very close to me I showed it the South.

It gripped me by the middle of my body, lifted me from the ground and placed me gently on its back. Lianas and thick leaves were fastened there; it was a bed of repose. While I was examining it I felt something touch my shoulder; it was my scimitar, which it had picked up and which it was holding out to me.

I lay down, and fitted myself, in order not to fall, with long lianas that were hanging down its flanks; once firmly attached, being fatigued, I went to sleep, after having marked in my memory the point of the Notion where I had stopped before that incident.

When I awoke the sun was at the zenith; palm trees and an Oriental city rose up in the solitude on the horizon. I was in Asiatic

Turkey; it was Bagdad. I untied the lianas around my limbs and my back It picked me up as it had the previous day—I say "the previous day" but I don't know how long my slumber lasted, perhaps two or three days— and placed me gently on the ground. I made it a sign that it could quit me; it disappeared, leaving me at the gates of Bagdad.

The simoom was blowing ardently; I took a few steps and lay down next to a fountain. An Armenian woman gave me a drink. That evening I found myself in the palace of Sheikh Ismail, near bazaars; we talked about the sovereignty of the Pashalik of Bagdad, which is already almost independent of the govern-ment of the Sublime Gate. I also talked to him about Europe. Ben-Ismail was full of distinction and amiability.

Tullia Fabriana closed the book.

"What's the point?" she said. "Can I forget?"

She got up, replaced the somber journal in the secret compartment, and the curtain fell back. The marchesa returned to the sphinx; she remained standing this time, her head tilted, her eyelids lowered.

Evidently, although her face had no expression, her soul was darkened terribly; she was dreaming.

Chapter XIV

The Eternal Feminine

The dancing water, the singing apple and
the little bird that says everything.
(Perrault)[1]

"Now," she said, "toward what precise and absolute
goal ought the deployment of my will, the expansion of my strength and the determination of my
intelligence extend?

"I know that the triumph of vast designs does not
depend on what they can resent of the stable and the
elevated; the dream must be incarnate in the execution,
in the cold mechanism of the accomplishment, and it
is the results that assign it its value; the ideal has no
other judge than itself. Everyone has an ideal; everyone
ought to do everything, brave everything and sacrifice
everything in order to accomplish it. All dreams are

---

1 The credit is mistaken; the three cited items are featured in a story
by Madame d'Aulnoy, "La Princesse Belle-Étoile et le prince Chéri"
(tr. as "Princess Belle-Étoile and Prince Cheri.")

equivalent; success poses the exterior value; but if the past is nothing, what, then, is happening? It is to be incapable of defining a single thought.

"I know the goal, and with regard to the execution, I need not, thus far, reproach myself for negligence. I have marched, in accordance with the laws of necessity, toward its complete realization. For what do I hope? Who will judge me among those who breathe? What mouth under the sun can proffer a terrible anathema against me?

"Oh, the nocturnal guest has not come to sup with me in Emmaus; he has not let the formulae of mercy fall upon my head; he has not transfigured the hills of Zion before me! And yet, Son of Man, I too have drunk the water of the torrent. The living have cast their shadow over the one who speaks alone in the darkness. Like you, I have gazed mildly at the suffering and the weak; like you, Emmanuel, I have been tempted on the mountain. You know by what acts and meditations I too have sanctified the day of the Sabbath; you know whether, like you, I have foreseen everything, as much as was possible for me, in order that everything might be accomplished."

Her voice was like the guttural breath of a limpid and harmonious equality; it mingled several languages without paying attention. She was speaking so softly that it would have been impossible to distinguish a single word a few feet from the sphinx. She did not appear to be moved, except that the gleam of her eyes was lost inside, to the point of rendering their expression atonal.

"It was not a man—a man having five or six thousand years of beliefs in his veins and who, supposing himself to be thinking alone, only accepted the Force in order to distract himself? Futile. It would have fatigued me to have him massacred in the subterrains with ax-blows by my Faces of lead on the eve of a coronation. It was a child that I desired: proud eyes, rich blood, a pure forehead, consciousness—yes, that was it.

"Spirits," she said, "you know it. When the thought came to me that I might be useful, I was about to anticipate the Hour and quit this world, where only the hope of being interested in something had retained me until then. I had pressed the sphere of exterior dreams, and its two poles, icy or torrid, seemed sterile to me. No magnet attracted me; the tranquility of those whose movement passes unperceived by themselves and who, fulfilling the métier that gives them bread, remain dissatisfied with having come—oh, that tranquility, I could not feel. My gaze only paused at intervals, chilled again, on the forms of a nature that no longer touched me. The unique and fixed thought of suicide was coiled and enlaced around me like a snake around a marble statue. Nothing seemed to me to be worth the trouble of a palpitation; I could only see the impassive Becoming. The insects that I crushed without knowing it as I walked, the funereal sweat and suffering of my fellows, the cost of the condition to which I was bound, the beings whose death, privations or toil were fatally necessary to my futile breath, excited too little enthusiasm in me for me not to 'do myself justice' by quitting them.

"However, as you know, by virtue of a supreme concession, I did not despair of a sensation in rapport with my mind and able to interest it in the depths of its sovereign disenchantment. Spirits! I asked it of you, but as it might be a favor . . ."

A curtain was moved aside by a white arm; it was Xoryl. She approached Tullia Fabriana and held out an enameled tray.

"Here are two letters," she said. "The violet armory was brought by the secretary of the papal legate—His Eminence's regrets and chagrin, etc.—and the note with a black seal by a lackey in livery of mourning."

The marchesa took the two letters.

The child withdrew.

Tullia Fabriana looked at the black seal with a certain attention.

She scanned the other letter, which she dropped, and she continued:

". . . dangerous to me, since it would be a momentary limit, I abstained from employing on my own authority the signs that inhibit Nature and whose effects are no longer suspended. I submitted that vague, unique and last desire to you, assigning you a term after which I would cease to await its accomplishment. If, within the indicated delay, that sensation were not granted to me, I would think it unimportant whether the last sheet of the veil were snatched away for me here. You know that; inasmuch as, clad in an organism of the human species, I am dependent on all the laws that, stemming from infinite relationships, come to intersect around my will, and I had fixed a day to finish with them absolutely.

"So, this evening, enclosed in the thundering blaze of this palace. I was going to drink the dust of my ring. Let the wind disperse the ungraspable atoms of my body, let the shadow receive the lines of my form, let my spirit reenter the divine annihilation of its unity—such were, for me, the decisions dictated by veritable wisdom.

"But, Spirits, you have wanted to satisfy the desire of the woman who speaks to you, and you have sent the man for whom I was waiting. I did not seek him, I did not want to seek him. Ought he not to come of his own accord and in his own time? Oh, the Child! I am pleased to strew his path, in advance, with the things most attractive for children, being sure that he would come sooner or later, in accordance with ancient presentiments! I thank you, sublime Spirits, who preside over the determinations of all virtuality, I thank you for having chosen yourselves and brought that amiable creature on the eve of the prescribed day! I congratulate you and I am very glad of his beauty, but his soul is new and profound; it only asks to be filled and to live!

"What treasures of celestial ingenuousness that utterly gracious intelligence must possess! Everything that he sees is covered by a prism of radiance and insouciance; it is like one of those virgin forests of the Ideal in which the first voyager, as soon as his first step and his first song, is welcomed by the enchanted concerts of its breezes, its flowers and its birds, emerging from the thousand echoes of its thickets, its rivers and its harmonious depths.

"What is going to happen now, powers that are interested in the determined movement of the heavens, because of the suffering that it signifies?

"I do not think it unknown.

"The first thing that will happen is that the child will see me through his own eyes and in his own way; in reality, I will only be an opportunity for the deployment of his thought; he will create and ineffable and indescribably being in my regard, and that phantom, ornamented with all the vivid notions appropriate to it, of absolute beauty, will be the mediator that he will mistake for me. What he will love will not be me, such as I am, but the person of his thought that I will appear to him to be. Doubtless he will accord me a thousand qualities and a thousand foreign charms, with which I would be unsatisfied if I had them; with the result that, believing that he possesses me, he will not even really touch me.

"That is the law of beings whose mental gaze does not surpass the sphere of possibilities, forms and hopes; they cannot emerge from themselves in their mysterious amours.

"To efface that relationship, in such a way that we can come together as we are, in Spirit, that is the solution to the first aspect of the problem.

"For that, I must genuinely become his vision; he will love my reflection; it is necessary that I animate that reflection by realizing it impersonally, by breaking the bars of its prison and refilling its hourglass with mine. I need to be dead to him first, and to survive his version of me.

"If I tried to reveal the truth to him, I would pass alongside him in parallel forever, because that truth, instantly modified by his mind, would no longer be what it ought to be. He would only comprehend it in accordance with some circle, and then he would be right not to love it any longer. It would sadden him because it would no longer appear to correspond with the vision he conceived, with the ideal to which he gave my name. It is therefore necessary that I am careful to reform that vision, by obscure transitions, as far as reality. It is necessary that his ideal is magnified by an ensemble of new reflections in order to reach the point of view where I am. Then it will be given to him to see the person who attracts him.

"If I had time to spare, I would almost regret not being able to love.

"In any case, is that any more than preserving for as long as possible the beautiful, very young life of lessening ennuis? Is it anything more than considering the noblest thing in the world, being moved, admiring, being astonished, dreaming, palpitating for an image, for an enchantment, for something shiny that enraptures those who cannot yet *see*? It's said. I shall try to live for an instant.

"Pardon me, you who do not deign to live, if I dare to advance in him the proof of the mission that is assigned to me. Why have I been preferred, if not to render this child the most ideally satisfied of all those who are and will be on this speck of extinct dust? To him, then, scepters, baubles and glorious crowns! To him, power, amour, youth and hectic shudders! To him the largest share of the sunlight of the living! To me the placid contemplation of all the beauties he will see—that he will create—in those things, since I consent to gaze at life through his eyes for a few moments!

"Then, when the first and inevitable circle of Form is surpassed, when I am sure of having enabled him to climb the steps of the supernatural world and that the words I pronounce, having no other meaning for him than the meaning of their expression, will not change in a thousand ways in his mind—then, the time will have come for Action! His throne, seated on the subterranean struggle that I shall sustain, will cover Italy, and from there . . . it will not be the first time that Italy will extend across the globe. One day, perhaps, thanks to a woman who will pass unknown . . . does not nature belong to anyone who can take it? What is impossible?

"Yes, my gaze has often penetrated centuries, climes and ages; I have seen the pages of the Future; I have understood the fateful times glimpsed by the inspired Skalds who sang in the mountains of Scandinavia; their songs, inscribed and conserved in runes in the sagas of the North, speak of warriors seated among the Aesir in the divine Valhalla. Are there not men bathing in glory and in the sap of the world, in the midst of torrents that reflect suns, and refreshing their immortal brows during wild nights in which the tempest sings to the breath of *the formless god*?"

She lowered her head and dreamed profoundly.

Nine o'clock sounded in the distance.

"I am not hesitating," she said.

And she added: "You, remember."

She waited, silent and concentrated, for a few minutes; her eyelids were closed, but she was not asleep.

"He is coming . . ." she said, again.

And, after a silence, she murmured, with her lips alone:

"He is here."

Chapter XV

Cras ingens iterabimus aequor[1]

"SIGNOR the Count of Strally-d'Anthas," Xoryl came to announce in a low voice.

The night-light being extinct, she placed a lamp on the table.

Wilhelm appeared on the threshold; she left, the curtain fell back.

Elegance is a strength. In accordance with the admirable fashion of the time, he was wearing a costume of black velvet, embroidered at the waist with delicate gold trimmings, and a choice épée. The white plume in his toque was secured by a precious stone; his gloves and boots allowed well-bred hands and feet to be divined. His black hair was disposed well over his forehead.

He had expressive dark blue eyes, brilliant with life; an elevated soul was already painted therein, and a penetrating intelligence. His straight nose gave him the

---

1 "Tomorrow, the wide seas." The quotation is taken from one of the Odes of Horace.

facial angle of the Roman type; his teeth and the whiteness of his skin were emphasized by the black down that shone on his upper lip. The arch of his black eyebrows was pronounced. He was well-made; his tall stature and the suppleness of his movements announced a developed vigor and athletic muscles.

As if to soften the severe beauty of his face, his smile had a child-like modesty and timidity. That was an august thing: men of great value sometimes veil themselves with that charitable smile; then it has an overwhelming force, and that humility is better evidence, for clear-sighted minds, of what we willingly call the power of the horizon, than any possible arrogance.

In sum, Count Wilhelm seemed to have no thought that was not benevolent and ingenuous.

Once, such a child represented the highest affirmation of human dignity. It required centuries to arrive at the production of his individuality. It was the result of the noble deeds and the integral probity of a series of ancestors whose glorious history and domestic virtues were evoked by his name. It was a living encouragement to perseverance, an emulation given to families. Today, the financial organizations under which the providential phenomenon of the first occupant always appear, a phenomenon uncontrollable in spite of its illegality, since it imposes itself by force as the principle of all right until the present, the declassification of people and the cult of progressive excellence have destroyed that social grandeur in most places, and will end up destroying it completely.

But we have something better. It is permitted to us to salute, in this century, a youth recognized almost universally for the rectitude of its mores, the frankness of its bearing and the nobility of its works. What a triumph for families is a generation of such high hopes!

Praise God, the health that reigns in the amours of today promises admirable virilities; it will doubtless resemble the growth of luxuriant tropical vegetation.

Slightly disconcerted by the dim light spread by the lamp and the furniture of the drawing room, the young man took a few steps toward Tullia Fabriana.

"Madame Marchesa," he said, "I have recalled constantly, since yesterday the permission that you deigned to grant me . . ."

And he bowed.

She extended her fingertips to him, very graciously, to brush with a kiss.

"Sit down, Count; I'm alone, as you see."

He advanced to one of the double cushions, of Arabic form and ornamentation, and then he looked at her

"The Prince must have departed last night," the marchesa continued, "but you still have a beautiful friend, the Duchess of Esperia. She's a very amiable person, is she not, Signor?"

Her abandoned pose and her tranquil tone had moved the young man, but he wanted to appear cool, for fear of displeasing.

"Do I not owe seeing you to her, Madame?" he replied.

She slowly lowered her gaze upon him; that was a decision.

Last night counted for years, she thought; *it's not only fever that animates those calmer eyes; there's the trace already left by the first dreams of passion, which can only be extinguished by a religious scorn. That's good.*

Her soul soared amid her thoughts like an eagle in the darkness; but, sure of bringing in a blissful fashion the instant she desired, she judged it pointless to defer it.

"An opera by Cimarosa is being performed this evening; you've sacrificed that marvelous music for me?"

"I'm hearing you speak, Madame," he said, in a slightly tremulous voice.

The affinities of the voice and thought, the transitions of which she was able to distinguish by means of an intuitive magnetism, revealed to her the feverish and naïve comedy that the count was striving to play, and, unafflicted by it, she forgave him sympathetically for that innocence of compliments and their transparent politeness. The young man appeared, in the style of society, to be "paying court to her"; but his voice, unintentionally, was expressing the profound emotion that he was feeling.

"Are you a musician, Signor Count?" she said

"Often," replied Wilhelm, with a sentiment of melancholy, "after a day of hunting and fatigue, when I come back late and I'm alone in the mountains, I sing to abridge the route."

The young man did not perceive the eccentricity of his response.

"Well," said Tullia Fabriana, "when you came in, I was looking at that harp." He turned round and saw, close to him, a large black harp that he was astonished not to have noticed when he sat down. "It's an admirable instrument, but I'm a little tired; sing a little German song, will you?"

Those few words, recited with inflexions of an enchanting coldness, produced an effect on Wilhelm that was translated by a dazzle and a pallor.

The marchesa got up; she approached the window in her white garments, supporting with one arm the wisps of batiste over her breast. The beautiful curls of her golden hair scarcely rose up in the warm breeze; the murmur of dense and perfumed foliage was audible; no nightingale was singing. A stroke of a bell, announcing prayer and slumber, rang out in the distance at the monastery of San Marco.

"What tranquility in the sky!" she said, softly; and after a momentary silence: "A spring night! Do you know anything about the night, Count?"

"Here's one, Madame."

And he sang:

The night to brilliant mystery
Opens her blue screens;
As many flowers are on earth
As there are stars in the sky.

One sees her dormant shadows
Brightening continually
As much by the charming flowers
As by the charming stars.

My night with a somber veil
Has only for charm and light
But one flower and one star:
My amour and your beauty!

It was a slow and gentle melody, but something entirely unexpected altered its simplicity.

At the first notes, a profound murmur ran around the strings of the harp, it was stirred by insensible vibrations, and suddenly, the meaning of the ballad seemed to him to be deformed by an unknown significance; his song hollowed out a turbulence around him.

The singular words that they had just exchanged, the somber richness that surrounded them, the black forms that Wilhelm distinguished vaguely on the ceiling without being able to explain what they were, the lividity that his ungloved hand had taken on as it leaned on the edge of the ebony table, the enormous head of the sphinx, framed by ribbons of stone, whose immobile eyes were fixed on him, the attractions of the woman who transported him with amour, and who, merely with the profound harmonies of her voice, caused his heart to beat frenetically, all formed the ensemble of some magnificent Oriental dream like one of the fictions created by reading the suras of the Koran in which the prophet speaks of mysterious pavilions and peris. He shivered, and his eyes closed at the final strophe.

A few moments later, when he opened his eyes again, his gaze fell on the lamp. It focused upon the light reflected by the golden vases, with a painful sentiment of solitude.

What, then, had happened?

Like the Sinbad of the legends of Asia, the young man was transported into the land of magic, dreams, marvels and presentiments. The immense chamber resembled the one into which Queen Cleopatra allowed those she remarked to enter; behind the door the great Nubian executioner with muscles of bronze and the dangerous ax was waiting. The perfumers of antique charmers, a rich and subtle aroma, a scent of balms, styrax and roses, stunned him.

And a Vision, fulgurant in relief and depth, rose before his eyes:

It seemed to him that the palace had become very ancient; ivy covered its collapsed front; its ruined façades were covered by moss; however, the old being still recalled its form; it was that of a supine man, his limbs extended, on a mountain. Prey to distant desolations, the Night now took charge of burying him in its shroud; the sky, a mortuary sheet strewn with great tears of fire that rolled incessantly down its face, was cast over his solitude; for him too Annihilation was building, in its imperative eternity, its vague mausoleum of forgetfulness. And the old palace resembled one of those giants whose beards and hair grow in the tomb.

But if he stood up, somber and devastated, the gardens were resplendent in the moonlight! The trees and the flowers had a magical beauty; in the distance, in a deep pond, Tullia Fabriana was bathing in the midst of crystal waters.

It was really her; her long hair was unfurled over her nacreous back; the moonbeams filtering through the cypresses shone over her entirety, and she seemed, at times, a fascinating siren of dark hours, flexing herself with delectable movements, in a vapor of diamonds. Swans, attracted by her whiteness, came to polish their wings against her flanks and her arms; he saw himself, pale, with his eyes closed, swimming next to the marchesa, and setting foot on the marble steps in order to emerge from the pool with her. And the Vision continued.

They were walking together now along the pathways. Immense lilacs swayed above their heads, their large clusters moist and dark; the air was embalmed by the vast shade of hornbeams. They walked, interlaced, under the gilded gaze of the stars; reawakened greyhounds and roe deer came to play around them at their feet; their nudity stood out under the leaves like that of a couple of antique marbles. One might have thought that they were two garden statues taking advantage of the darkness to come to life. Their lips sometimes touched silently in the shadow, and they understood one another without speaking.

And, pulling the petals from the white roses on the shoulders of the great enchantress, he said to her:

"Your amour is a sky of which I had no suspicion; a kiss from you is the infinity!"

She did not reply, but she made him a sign, slowly, to look at what was happening.

Their bodies were attenuated to the point of becoming phantoms; a muted oscillation agitated the metallic depths of nature; the relief of everything was gradually effaced, as when one dies; the Vision became shadow and fluid, and everything disappeared into the empire of Nirvana.

Count Wilhelm passed his hand over his forehead and returned to the window.

The obscurity of the night had deepened outside; there was no rustle of foliage in the gardens, no breath of air came into the apartment through the wide opened casement.

Without taking account of his movement he tried to look at the sky; it was no longer there. The night was completely black, and there was an extraordinary silence, a silence of abstraction, in which the last vibrations of the harp were dying, faintly and harmoniously . . .

It was then that he forgot living slightly in order to reflect involuntarily, and dared to look ahead of him.

Between the elevated vault of the apartment and his feet, the atmosphere was divided into two absolutely disparate zones.

The light of the lamp illuminated him and the entire part in which he was located; and he appeared in a radiant effusion. The part where Tullia Fabriana ought to be was rolling a reflux of shadows; there were waves of obscurity, heavy and, above all, seemingly distant. He could not see either the sphinx or the woman. He took a step; he perceived the caryatids and he seemed to see their terrible eyes stirring. In spite of his legible forehead and his young smile, it seemed to him that it was not yesterday that he had experienced the vertiginous sentiment of life, and that he had suffered magnificently once, in the past.

Then, with a bewildered gesture, as if moving aside a curtain of darkness, he entered, tottering, into vast shadows.

And he saw, rising up slowly in front of him, in the same shadows, something like another gesture enveloped with veils; he had the impression of two arms coming together—oh, dolorously!—around his neck. A form of radiant whiteness drew his forehead toward it . . . and there was a swarm of infinite pale joys, the tremor of divine dreams, torture . . .

That evening, the Count of Strally-d'Anthas spent the night with the Marchesa Tullia Fabriana.

Printed in the USA
CPSIA information can be obtained
at www.ICGtesting.com
LVHW092256181123
764329LV00006B/991

9 781645 250043